I0884830

New Testament Studies

IV

THE DATE OF THE ACTS AND OF THE SYNOPTIC GOSPELS

BY

ADOLF HARNACK

PROFESSOR OF CHURCH HISTORY IN THE UNIVERSITY OF BERLIN

TRANSLATED BY

THE REV. J. R. WILKINSON, M.A.

LATE SCHOLAR OF WORCESTER COLLEGE, OXFORD; AND RECTOR OF WINFORD

Wipf & Stock
PUBLISHERS
Eugene, Oregon

Wipf and Stock Publishers
199 West 8th Avenue, Suite 3
Eugene, Oregon 97401

The Date of Acts and the Synoptic Gospels
By Harnack, Adolf
ISBN: 1-59244-569-1
Publication date 2/25/2004
Previously published by Williams and Norgate, 1911

CONTENTS

DATE OF THE ACTS AND THE SYNOPTIC GOSPELS

CHAPTER I

THE IDENTITY OF THE AUTHOR OF THE "WE"-SECTIONS OF THE ACTS OF THE APOSTLES WITH THE AUTHOR OF THE WHOLE WORK

One of the strongest arguments in favour of this identity is the argument from *language* and *style*. In my two earlier works (*Luke the Physician* and *The Acts of the Apostles*) I have presented this argument in full detail, and it is to be hoped have proved conclusively that the hypothesis of a difference of authors is untenable. We are here concerned not only with a striking agreement in the use of words, but with an agreement in syntax and style which is just as striking, and above all with an identity of interest which extends into the minutest details of the narrative, such as the literary treatment of persons, lands, cities, peoples, houses, dates, etc., and which shows itself even in similar instances of carelessness and petty discrepancy. But a certain number of critics still regard the proof as unsatisfactory. Thus Paul Wilhelm Schmidt[1] declares that "linguistic

[1] *Festschrift zur Feier des 450-jahr. Bestehens der Univ. Basel* (De Wette-Overbeck's Werk zur Apostelgesch. und dessen jüngste Bestreitung), 1910, S. 44.

homogeneity is not the same thing as linguistic identity; between even St Luke's gospel of the Childhood, especially the Magnificat and Benedictus on the one hand, and the rest of the gospel of St Luke on the other hand, there exists, as Harnack has lately shown, a far-reaching linguistic harmony." But it is just identity, and not merely homogeneity, which is disclosed by our researches into St Luke's language and style; and the gospel of the Childhood, including the two canticles, is shown to be no source which, like the supposed "diary of travel," has been incorporated into his work, but either a free elaboration of oral tradition or a free translation of an Aramaic record. From the study of the source Q in the gospel we can learn how a source that has been adopted by St Luke stands out from his own work. Of the 261 words which occur in the New Testament only in the gospel of St Luke, 3 at the most are to be found in the sections of the gospel derived from Q[1]! Compare with this the vocabulary of the "we"-sections in its relation to that of the whole Acts of the Apostles! Is not this in itself enough to convince any critic that the "we"-sections could not have been an independent source? But how much easier it is to obtain credence for some questionable hypothesis than to gain acceptance for what admits of stringent logical demonstration! So it has ever been, and so it will ever be! It is the same with Clemen. Again the proof based upon language and style makes no impression. He writes[2]—all is

[1] *Sayings of Jesus*, Preface.

[2] "Professor Harnack on Acts" (*Hibbert Journal*, viii. 4, 1910, July, p. 787).

explained "partly from the fact that these details are historical and therefore could be mentioned by various writers, partly from the terminology common to the whole book of Acts." This is a way out of the difficulty that can be acquiesced in only by one who has not studied in detail the actual nature of the coincidences and is content to quiet his intellectual conscience with preconceived opinions.[1]

Seeing that so much depends upon the argument in question, I have now determined to lay before my readers the whole material upon which it is based. In my treatise *Luke the Physician* (pp. 40–65) I verse by verse pointed out the linguistic coincidences in the passages Acts xvi. 10–17 and xxviii. 1–16, and then gave a summary description (pp. 67–84) of the vocabulary of the "we"-sections in comparison with the whole Acts of the Apostles. I shall now in the following pages print the whole text of the "we"-sections, underlining those words or constructions which occur again in the Acts and in the gospel of St Luke, while in the rest of the historical books of the New Testament they find either no parallel or one of a slight description.[2] From

[1] I am the more pleased to find that Moulton, the foremost authority on New Testament Greek, upholds the unity of authorship. He writes (*A Grammar of the New Testament*,[3] 1908, p. 14): "I was quite content to shield myself behind Blass; but Harnack has now stepped in with decisive effect. The following pages will supply not a few grammatical points to supplement Harnack's stylistic evidence in *Luke the Physician*." As a matter of fact, Moulton has himself noticed a whole series of delicate stylistic traits which confirm the unity of authorship.

[2] We add a few other peculiarities which the "we"-sections share with the whole book of the Acts, apart altogether from the gospels.

considerations of space I may be allowed to omit a commentary on these passages, such as that which I have given upon ch. xvi. 10–17 and xxviii. 1–6. The principles in accordance with which the passages are selected remain exactly the same; and the careful reader, with the help of a concordance—the commentaries, with the exception of that of B. Weiss, will often fail him—will easily be able to ascertain in each particular case the reason why a particular word or construction is underlined. It is obvious that the distinction by underlining is not always of the same value, but it is impossible to represent in print different degrees of importance, especially when in many cases the valuation cannot be other than subjective.

xvi. 10–17.

10 Ὡς δὲ τὸ ὅραμα εἶδεν, εὐθέως ἐζητήσαμεν ἐξελθεῖν
εἰς Μακεδονίαν, συμβιβάζοντες ὅτι προσκέκληται ἡμᾶς
ὁ θεὸς εὐαγγελίσασθαι αὐτούς. 11 ἀναχθέντες δὲ ἀπὸ
Τρῳάδος εὐθυδρομήσαμεν εἰς Σαμαθρᾴκην, τῇ δὲ ἐπιούσῃ
εἰς Νέαν Πόλιν, 12 κἀκεῖθεν εἰς Φιλίππους, ἥτις ἐστὶν
πρώτη τῆς μερίδος τῆς Μακεδονίας πόλις, κολωνία.
ἦμεν δὲ ἐν ταύτῃ τῇ πόλει διατρίβοντες ἡμέρας τινάς.
13 τῇ τε ἡμέρᾳ τῶν σαββάτων ἐξήλθομεν ἔξω τῆς πύλης
παρὰ ποταμόν, οὗ ἐνομίζομεν προσευχὴν εἶναι, καὶ
καθίσαντες ἐλαλοῦμεν ταῖς συνελθούσαις γυναιξίν. 14 καί
τις γυνὴ ὀνόματι Λυδία, πορφυρόπωλις πόλεως Θυατείρων,
σεβομένη τὸν θεόν, ἤκουεν, ἧς ὁ κύριος διήνοιξεν τὴν καρδίαν
προσέχειν τοῖς λαλουμένοις ὑπὸ Παύλου. 15 ὡς δὲ
ἐβαπτίσθη καὶ ὁ οἶκος αὐτῆς, παρεκάλεσεν λέγουσα· εἰ
κεκρίκατέ με πιστὴν τῷ κυρίῳ εἶναι, εἰσελθόντες εἰς τὸν

οἶκόν μου μένετε· καὶ παρεβιάσατο ἡμᾶς. 16 ἐγένετο δέ,
πορευομένων ἡμῶν εἰς τὴν προσευχήν, παιδίσκην τινὰ
ἔχουσαν πνεῦμα πύθωνα ὑπαντῆσαι ἡμῖν, ἥτις ἐργασίαν
πολλὴν παρεῖχεν τοῖς κυρίοις αὐτῆς μαντευομένη. 17 αὕτη
κατακολουθοῦσα τῷ Παύλῳ καὶ ἡμῖν ἔκραζεν λέγουσα·
οὗτοι οἱ ἄνθρωποι δοῦλοι τοῦ θεοῦ τοῦ ὑψίστου εἰσίν,
οἵτινες καταγγέλλουσιν ὑμῖν ὁδὸν σωτηρίας. τοῦτο δὲ
ἐποίει ἐπὶ πολλὰς ἡμέρας.

xx. 4–16; xxi. 1–18.

4 Συνείπετο δὲ αὐτῷ [Παύλῳ] Σώπατρος Πύρρου
Βεροιαῖος, Θεσσαλονικέων δὲ Ἀρίσταρχος καὶ Σεκοῦνδος
καὶ Γάϊος Δερβαῖος καὶ Τιμόθεος, Ἀσιανοὶ δὲ Τύχικος
καὶ Τρόφιμος. 5 οὗτοι δὲ προελθόντες ἔμενον ἡμᾶς ἐν
Τρῳάδι. 6 ἡμεῖς δὲ ἐξεπλεύσαμεν μετὰ τὰς ἡμέρας τῶν
ἀζύμων ἀπὸ Φιλίππων καὶ ἤλθομεν πρὸς αὐτοὺς εἰς τὴν
Τρῳάδα ἄχρι ἡμερῶν πέντε, οὗ διετρίψαμεν ἡμέρας ἑπτά.
7 ἐν δὲ τῇ μιᾷ τῶν σαββάτων συνηγμένων ἡμῶν κλάσαι
ἄρτον ὁ Παῦλος διελέγετο αὐτοῖς, μέλλων ἐξιέναι τῇ
ἐπαύριον, παρέτεινέν τε τὸν λόγον μέχρι μεσονυκτίου.
8 ἦσαν δὲ λαμπάδες ἱκαναὶ ἐν τῷ ὑπερῴῳ, οὗ ἦμεν συνηγ-
μένοι. 9 καθεζόμενος δέ τις νεανίας ὀνόματι Εὔτυχος
ἐπὶ τῆς θυρίδος, καταφερόμενος ὕπνῳ βαθεῖ, διαλεγομένου
τοῦ Παύλου ἐπὶ πλεῖον, κατενεχθεὶς ἀπὸ τοῦ ὕπνου
ἔπεσεν ἀπὸ τοῦ τριστέγου κάτω καὶ ἤρθη νεκρός.
10 καταβὰς δὲ ὁ Παῦλος ἐπέπεσεν αὐτῷ καὶ συνπεριλαβὼν
εἶπεν· μὴ θορυβεῖσθε. ἡ γὰρ ψυχὴ αὐτοῦ ἐν αὐτῷ ἐστιν.
11 ἀναβὰς δὲ καὶ κλάσας τὸν ἄρτον καὶ γευσάμενος. ἐφ'
ἱκανόν τε ὁμιλήσας ἄχρι αὐγῆς, οὕτως ἐξῆλθεν. 12 ἤγαγον
δὲ τὸν παῖδα ζῶντα, καὶ παρεκλήθησαν οὐ μετρίως.

[13] ἡμεῖς δὲ προσελθόντες ἐπὶ τὸ πλοῖον ἀνήχθημεν ἐπὶ
τὴν Ἄσσον, ἐκεῖθεν μέλλοντες ἀναλαμβάνειν τὸν Παῦλον·
οὕτως γὰρ διατεταγμένος ἦν, μέλλων αὐτὸς πεζεύειν.
[14] ὡς δὲ συνέβαλλεν ἡμῖν εἰς τὴν Ἄσσον, ἀναλαβόντες
αὐτὸν ἤλθομεν εἰς Μιτυλήνην. [15] κἀκεῖθεν ἀποπλεύσαντες
τῇ ἐπιούσῃ κατηντήσαμεν ἄντικρυς Χίου, τῇ δὲ ἑσπέρᾳ
παρεβάλομεν εἰς Σάμον, καὶ μείναντες ἐν Τρωγιλίᾳ τῇ
ἐχομένῃ ἤλθομεν εἰς Μίλητον· [16] κεκρίκει γὰρ ὁ Παῦλος
παραπλεῦσαι τὴν Ἔφεσον, ὅπως μὴ γένηται αὐτῷ
χρονοτριβῆσαι ἐν τῇ Ἀσίᾳ· ἔσπευδεν γάρ, εἰ δυνατὸν
εἴη αὐτῷ, τὴν ἡμέραν τῆς πεντηκοστῆς γενέσθαι εἰς
Ἱεροσόλυμα . . . .

xxi. [1] Ὡς δὲ ἐγένετο ἀναχθῆναι ἡμᾶς ἀποσπασθέντας
ἀπ᾽ αὐτῶν, εὐθυδρομήσαντες ἤλθομεν εἰς τὴν Κῶ, τῇ δὲ
ἑξῆς εἰς τὴν Ῥόδον, κἀκεῖθεν εἰς Πάταρα. [2] καὶ εὑρόντες
πλοῖον διαπερῶν εἰς Φοινίκην, ἐπιβάντες ἀνήχθημεν.
[3] ἀναφάναντες δὲ τὴν Κύπρον καὶ καταλιπόντες αὐτὴν
εὐώνυμον ἐπλέομεν εἰς Συρίαν, καὶ κατήλθομεν εἰς Τύρον.
ἐκεῖσε γὰρ τὸ πλοῖον ἦν ἀποφορτιζόμενον τὸν γόμον.
[4] ἀνευρόντες δὲ τοὺς μαθητὰς ἐπεμείναμεν αὐτοῦ ἡμέρας
ἑπτά. οἵτινες τῷ Παύλῳ ἔλεγον διὰ τοῦ πνεύματος μὴ
ἐπιβαίνειν εἰς Ἱεροσόλυμα. [5] ὅτε δὲ ἐγένετο ἐξαρτίσαι
ἡμᾶς τὰς ἡμέρας, ἐξελθόντες ἐπορευόμεθα προπεμπόντων
ἡμᾶς πάντων σὺν γυναιξὶ καὶ τέκνοις ἕως ἔξω τῆς πόλεως,
καὶ θέντες τὰ γόνατα ἐπὶ τὸν αἰγιαλὸν προσευξάμενοι
[6] ἀπησπασάμεθα ἀλλήλους, καὶ ἐνέβημεν εἰς τὸ πλοῖον,
ἐκεῖνοι δὲ ὑπέστρεψαν εἰς τὰ ἴδια. [7] ἡμεῖς δὲ τὸν πλοῦν
διανύσαντες ἀπὸ Τύρου κατηντήσαμεν εἰς Πτολεμαΐδα,
καὶ ἀσπασάμενοι τοὺς ἀδελφοὺς ἐμείναμεν ἡμέραν μίαν
παρ᾽ αὐτοῖς. [8] τῇ δὲ ἐπαύριον ἐξελθόντες ἤλθομεν εἰς
Καισαρίαν, καὶ εἰσελθόντες εἰς τὸν οἶκον Φιλίππου τοῦ

εὐαγγελιστοῦ, ὄντος ἐκ τῶν ἑπτά, ἐμείναμεν παρ' αὐτῷ·
9 τούτῳ δὲ ἦσαν θυγατέρες τέσσαρες παρθένοι προ-
φητεύουσαι. 10 ἐπιμενόντων δὲ ἡμέρας πλείους κατῆλθέν
τις ἀπὸ τῆς Ἰουδαίας προφήτης ὀνόματι Ἄγαβος, 11 καὶ
ἐλθὼν πρὸς ἡμᾶς καὶ ἄρας τὴν ζώνην τοῦ Παύλου, δήσας
ἑαυτοῦ τοὺς πόδας καὶ τὰς χεῖρας εἶπεν· τάδε λέγει τὸ
πνεῦμα τὸ ἅγιον· τὸν ἄνδρα, οὗ ἐστιν ἡ ζώνη αὕτη, οὕτως
δήσουσιν ἐν Ἰερουσαλὴμ οἱ Ἰουδαῖοι καὶ παραδώσουσιν
εἰς χεῖρας ἐθνῶν. 12 ὡς δὲ ἠκούσαμεν ταῦτα, παρεκαλοῦμεν
ἡμεῖς τε καὶ οἱ ἐντόπιοι τοῦ μὴ ἀναβαίνειν αὐτὸν εἰς
Ἰερουσαλήμ. 13 τότε ἀπεκρίθη ὁ Παῦλος· τί ποιεῖτε
κλαίοντες καὶ συνθρύπτοντές μου τὴν καρδίαν; ἐγὼ γὰρ
οὐ μόνον δεθῆναι ἀλλὰ καὶ ἀποθανεῖν εἰς Ἰερουσαλὴμ
ἑτοίμως ἔχω ὑπὲρ τοῦ ὀνόματος τοῦ κυρίου Ἰησοῦ.
14 μὴ πειθομένου δὲ αὐτοῦ ἡσυχάσαμεν εἰπόντες· τοῦ
κυρίου τὸ θέλημα γινέσθω. 15 μετὰ δε τὰς ἡμέρας
ταύτας ἐπισκευασάμενοι ἀνεβαίνομεν εἰς Ἱεροσόλυμα.
16 συνῆλθον δὲ καὶ τῶν μαθητῶν ἀπὸ Καισαρίας σὺν
ἡμῖν, ἄγοντες παρ' ᾧ ξενισθῶμεν Μνάσωνί τινι Κυπρίῳ,
ἀρχαίῳ μαθητῇ. 17 γενομένων δὲ ἡμῶν εἰς Ἱεροσόλυμα
ἀσμένως ἀπεδέξαντο ἡμᾶς οἱ ἀδελφοί. 18 τῇ δὲ ἐπιούσῃ
εἰσῄει ὁ Παῦλος σὺν ἡμῖν πρὸς Ἰάκωβον, πάντες τε παρε-
γένοντο οἱ πρεσβύτεροι . . . .

xxvii. 1–xxviii. 16.

1 Ὡς δὲ ἐκρίθη τοῦ ἀποπλεῖν ἡμᾶς εἰς τὴν Ἰταλίαν,
παρεδίδουν τόν τε Παῦλον καί τινας ἑτέρους δεσμώτας
ἑκατοντάρχῃ ὀνόματι Ἰουλίῳ σπείρης Σεβαστῆς. 2 ἐπι-
βάντες δὲ πλοίῳ Ἀδραμυττηνῷ μέλλοντι πλεῖν εἰς τοὺς
κατὰ τὴν Ἀσίαν τόπους ἀνήχθημεν, ὄντος σὺν ἡμῖν

Ἀριστάρχου Μακεδόνος Θεσσαλονικέως· 3 τῇ τε ἑτέρᾳ
κατήχθημεν εἰς Σιδῶνα φιλανθρώπως τε ὁ Ἰούλιος τῷ
Παύλῳ χρησάμενος ἐπέτρεψεν πρὸς τοὺς φίλους πορευ-
θέντι ἐπιμελείας τυχεῖν. 4 κἀκεῖθεν ἀναχθέντες ὑπεπλεύ-
σαμεν τὴν Κύπρον διὰ τὸ τοὺς ἀνέμους εἶναι ἐναντίους,
5 τό τε πέλαγος τὸ κατὰ τὴν Κιλικίαν καὶ Παμφυλίαν
διαπλεύσαντες κατήλθαμεν εἰς Μύρρα τῆς Λυκίας. 6 κἀκεῖ
εὑρὼν ὁ ἑκατοντάρχης πλοῖον Ἀλεξανδρινὸν πλέον εἰς
τὴν Ἰταλίαν ἐνεβίβασεν ἡμᾶς εἰς αὐτό. 7 ἐν ἱκαναῖς δὲ
ἡμέραις βραδυπλοοῦντες καὶ μόλις γενόμενοι κατὰ τὴν
Κνίδον, μὴ προσεῶντος ἡμᾶς τοῦ ἀνέμου, ὑπεπλεύσαμεν
τὴν Κρήτην κατὰ Σαλμώνην, 8 μόλις τε παραλεγόμενοι
αὐτὴν ἤλθομεν εἰς τόπον τινὰ καλούμενον Καλοὺς Λιμένας,
ᾧ ἐγγὺς ἦν πόλις Λασαία. 9 ἱκανοῦ δὲ χρόνου διαγενο-
μένου καὶ ὄντος ἤδη ἐπισφαλοῦς τοῦ πλοὸς διὰ τὸ καὶ
τὴν νηστείαν ἤδη παρεληλυθέναι, παρῄνει ὁ Παῦλος λέγων
αὐτοῖς· 10 ἄνδρες, θεωρῶ ὅτι μετὰ ὕβρεως καὶ πολλῆς
ζημίας οὐ μόνον τοῦ φορτίου καὶ τοῦ πλοίου ἀλλὰ καὶ
τῶν ψυχῶν ἡμῶν μέλλειν ἔσεσθαι τὸν πλοῦν. 11 ὁ δὲ
ἑκατοντάρχης τῷ κυβερνήτῃ καὶ τῷ ναυκλήρῳ μᾶλλον
ἐπείθετο ἢ τοῖς ὑπὸ Παύλου λεγομένοις. 12 ἀνευθέτου δὲ
τοῦ λιμένος ὑπάρχοντος πρὸς παραχειμασίαν οἱ πλείονες
ἔθεντο βουλὴν ἀναχθῆναι ἐκεῖθεν, εἴ πως δύναιντο καταν-
τήσαντες εἰς Φοίνικα παραχειμάσαι, λιμένα τῆς Κρήτης
βλέποντα κατὰ λίβα καὶ κατὰ χῶρον. 13 ὑποπνεύσαντος
δὲ νότου δόξαντες τῆς προθέσεως κεκρατηκέναι, ἄραντες
ἆσσον παρελέγοντο τὴν Κρήτην. 14 μετ' οὐ πολὺ δὲ
ἔβαλεν κατ' αὐτῆς ἄνεμος τυφωνικὸς ὁ καλούμενος εὐρα-
κύλων. 15 συναρπασθέντος δὲ τοῦ πλοίου καὶ μὴ δυναμένου
ἀντοφθαλμεῖν τῷ ἀνέμῳ ἐπιδόντες ἐφερόμεθα. 16 νησίον
δέ τι ὑποδραμόντες καλούμενον Κλαῦδα ἰσχύσαμεν μόλις

περικρατεῖς γενέσθαι τῆς σκάφης, 17 ἣν ἄραντες βοηθείαις
ἐχρῶντο, ὑποζωννύντες τὸ πλοῖον· φοβούμενοί τε μὴ εἰς
τὴν Σύρτιν ἐκπέσωσιν, χαλάσαντες τὸ σκεῦος, οὕτως
ἐφέροντο. 18 σφοδρῶς δὲ χειμαζομένων ἡμῶν τῇ ἑξῆς
ἐκβολὴν ἐποιοῦντο, 19 καὶ τῇ τρίτῃ αὐτόχειρες τὴν
σκευὴν τοῦ πλοίου ἔρριψαν. 20 μήτε ἡλίου μήτε ἄστρων
ἐπιφαινόντων ἐπὶ πλείονας ἡμέρας, χειμῶνός τε οὐκ
ὀλίγου ἐπικειμένου, λοιπὸν περιῃρεῖτο ἐλπὶς πᾶσα τοῦ
σώζεσθαι ἡμᾶς. 21 πολλῆς τε ἀσιτίας ὑπαρχούσης τότε
σταθεὶς ὁ Παῦλος ἐν μέσῳ αὐτῶν εἶπεν· ἔδει μέν, ὦ ἄνδρες,
πειθαρχήσαντάς μοι μὴ ἀνάγεσθαι ἀπὸ τῆς Κρήτης
κερδῆσαί τε τὴν ὕβριν ταύτην καὶ τὴν ζημίαν. 22 καὶ τὰ
νῦν παραινῶ ὑμᾶς εὐθυμεῖν· ἀποβολὴ γὰρ ψυχῆς οὐδεμία
ἔσται ἐξ ὑμῶν πλὴν τοῦ πλοίου. 23 παρέστη γάρ μοι
ταύτῃ τῇ νυκτὶ τοῦ θεοῦ, οὗ εἰμι, ᾧ καὶ λατρεύω, ἄγγελος
24 λέγων· μὴ φοβοῦ, Παῦλε· Καίσαρί σε δεῖ παραστῆναι,
καὶ ἰδοὺ κεχάρισταί σοι ὁ θεὸς πάντας τοὺς πλέοντας
μετὰ σοῦ. 25 διὸ εὐθυμεῖτε, ἄνδρες· πιστεύω γὰρ τῷ
θεῷ ὅτι οὕτως ἔσται καθ' ὃν τρόπον λελάληταί μοι.
26 εἰς νῆσον δέ τινα δεῖ ἡμᾶς ἐκπεσεῖν. 27 ὡς δὲ τεσσαρεσ-
καιδεκάτη νὺξ ἐγένετο διαφερομένων ἡμῶν ἐν τῷ Ἀδρίᾳ,
κατὰ μέσον τῆς νυκτὸς ὑπενόουν οἱ ναῦται προσάγειν
τινὰ αὐτοῖς χώραν. 28 καὶ βολίσαντες εὗρον ὀργυιὰς
εἴκοσι, βραχὺ δὲ διαστήσαντες καὶ πάλιν βολίσαντες
εὗρον ὀργυιὰς δεκαπέντε· 29 φοβούμενοί τε μή που
κατὰ τραχεῖς τόπους ἐκπέσωμεν, ἐκ πρύμνης ῥίψαντες
ἀγκύρας τέσσαρας εὔχοντο ἡμέραν γενέσθαι. 30 τῶν δε
ναυτῶν ζητούντων φυγεῖν ἐκ τοῦ πλοίου καὶ χαλασάντων
τὴν σκάφην εἰς τὴν θάλασσαν προφάσει ὡς ἐκ πρῴρης
ἀγκύρας μελλόντων ἐκτείνειν, 31 εἶπεν ὁ Παῦλος τῷ
ἑκατοντάρχῃ καὶ τοῖς στρατιώταις· ἐὰν μὴ οὗτοι μείνωσιν

ἐν τῷ πλοίῳ, ὑμεῖς σωθῆναι οὐ δύνασθε. 32 τότε ἀπέ-
κοψαν οἱ στρατιῶται τὰ σχοινία τῆς σκάφης καὶ εἴασαν
αὐτὴν ἐκπεσεῖν. 33 ἄχρι δὲ οὗ ἡμέρα ἤμελλεν γίνεσθαι,
παρεκάλει ὁ Παῦλος ἅπαντας μεταλαβεῖν τροφῆς λέγων·
τεσσαρεσκαιδεκάτην σήμερον ἡμέραν προσδοκῶντες ἄσιτοι
διατελεῖτε, μηδὲν προσλαβόμενοι. 34 διὸ παρακαλῶ ὑμᾶς
μεταλαβεῖν τροφῆς· τοῦτο γὰρ πρὸς τῆς ὑμετέρας
σωτηρίας ὑπάρχει· οὐδενὸς γὰρ ὑμῶν θρὶξ ἀπὸ τῆς
κεφαλῆς ἀπολεῖται. 35 εἴπας δὲ ταῦτα καὶ λαβὼν ἄρτον
εὐχαρίστησεν τῷ θεῷ ἐνώπιον πάντων καὶ κλάσας ἤρξατο
ἐσθίειν. 36 εὔθυμοι δὲ γενόμενοι πάντες καὶ αὐτοὶ προσ-
ελάβοντο τροφῆς. 37 ἤμεθα δὲ αἱ πᾶσαι ψυχαὶ ἐν
τῷ πλοίῳ διακόσιαι ἑβδομήκοντα ἕξ. 38 κορεσθέντες δὲ
τροφῆς ἐκούφιζον τὸ πλοῖον ἐκβαλλόμενοι τὸν σῖτον
εἰς τὴν θάλασσαν. 39 ὅτε δὲ ἡμέρα ἐγένετο, τὴν γῆν οὐκ
ἐπεγίνωσκον, κόλπον δέ τινα κατενόουν ἔχοντα αἰγιαλόν,
εἰς ὃν ἐβουλεύοντο εἰ δύναιντο ἐξῶσαι τὸ πλοῖον. 40 καὶ
τὰς ἀγκύρας περιελόντες εἴων εἰς τὴν θάλασσαν, ἅμα
ἀνέντες τὰς ζευκτηρίας τῶν πηδαλίων, καὶ ἐπάραντες
τὸν ἀρτέμωνα τῇ πνεούσῃ κατεῖχον εἰς τὸν αἰγιαλόν.
41 περιπεσόντες δὲ εἰς τόπον διθάλασσον ἐπέκειλαν τὴν
ναῦν, καὶ ἡ μὲν πρῷρα ἔμεινεν ἀσάλευτος, ἡ δὲ πρύμνα
ἐλύετο ὑπὸ τῆς βίας. 42 τῶν δὲ στρατιωτῶν βουλὴ
ἐγένετο ἵνα τοὺς δεσμώτας ἀποκτείνωσιν, μή τις ἐκκο-
λυμβήσας διαφύγῃ· 43 ὁ δὲ ἑκατοντάρχης βουλόμενος
διασῶσαι τὸν Παῦλον ἐκώλυσεν αὐτοὺς τοῦ βουλήματος,
ἐκέλευσέν τε τοὺς δυναμένους κολυμβᾶν ἀπορίψαντας
πρώτους ἐπὶ τὴν γῆν ἐξιέναι, 44 καὶ τοὺς λοιποὺς οὓς μὲν
ἐπὶ σανίσιν, οὓς δὲ ἐπί τινων τῶν ἀπὸ τοῦ πλοίου. καὶ
οὕτως ἐγένετο πάντας διασωθῆναι ἐπὶ τὴν γῆν.

xxviii. 1 καὶ διασωθέντες τότε ἐπέγνωμεν ὅτι Μελίτη

ἡ νῆσος καλεῖται. 2 οἵ τε βάρβαροι παρεῖχαν οὐ τὴν
τυχοῦσαν φιλανθρωπίαν ἡμῖν· ἅψαντες γὰρ πυρὰν προσ-
ελάβοντο πάντας ἡμᾶς διὰ τὸν ὑετὸν τὸν ἐφεστῶτα
καὶ διὰ τὸ ψῦχος. 3 συστρέψαντος δὲ τοῦ Παύλου
φρυγάνων τι πλῆθος καὶ ἐπιτιθέντος ἐπὶ τὴν πυρὰν
ἔχιδνα ἀπὸ τῆς θέρμης ἐξελθοῦσα καθῆψε τῆς χειρὸς
αὐτοῦ. 4 ὡς δὲ εἶδον οἱ βάρβαροι κρεμάμενον τὸ θηρίον
ἐκ τῆς χειρὸς αὐτοῦ, πρὸς ἀλλήλους ἔλεγον· πάντως
φονεύς ἐστιν ὁ ἄνθρωπος οὗτος, ὃν διασωθέντα ἐκ τῆς
θαλάσσης ἡ Δίκη ζῆν οὐκ εἴασεν. 5 ὁ μὲν οὖν ἀποτινάξας
τὸ θηρίον εἰς τὸ πῦρ ἔπαθεν οὐδὲν κακόν. 6 οἱ δὲ προ-
σεδόκων αὐτὸν μέλλειν πίμπρασθαι ἢ καταπίπτειν ἄφνω
νεκρόν. ἐπὶ πολὺ δὲ αὐτῶν προσδοκώντων καὶ θεωρούντων
μηδὲν ἄτοπον εἰς αὐτὸν γινόμενον μεταβαλόμενοι ἔλεγον
αὐτὸν εἶναι θεόν.

7 Ἐν δὲ τοῖς περὶ τὸν τόπον ἐκεῖνον ὑπῆρχεν χωρία
τῷ πρώτῳ τῆς νήσου, ὀνόματι Ποπλίῳ, ὃς ἀναδεξάμενος
ἡμᾶς ἡμέρας τρεῖς φιλοφρόνως ἐξένισεν. 8 ἐγένετο δὲ
τὸν πατέρα τοῦ Ποπλίου πυρετοῖς καὶ δυσεντερίῳ
συνεχόμενον κατακεῖσθαι, πρὸς ὃν ὁ Παῦλος εἰσελθὼν
καὶ προσευξάμενος, ἐπιθεὶς τὰς χεῖρας αὐτῷ, ἰάσατο
αὐτόν. 9 τούτου δὲ γενομένου καὶ οἱ λοιποὶ οἱ ἐν τῇ
νήσῳ ἔχοντες ἀσθενείας προσήρχοντο καὶ ἐθεραπεύοντο,
10 οἳ καὶ πολλαῖς τιμαῖς ἐτίμησαν ἡμᾶς καὶ ἀναγομένοις
ἐπέθεντο τὰ πρὸς τὰς χρείας.

11 Μετὰ δὲ τρεῖς μῆνας ἀνήχθημεν ἐν πλοίῳ παρακεχει-
μακότι ἐν τῇ νήσῳ, Ἀλεξανδρινῷ, παρασήμῳ Διοσκούροις,
12 καὶ καταχθέντες εἰς Συρακούσας ἐπεμείναμεν ἡμέραις
τρισίν, 13 ὅθεν περιελθόντες κατηντήσαμεν εἰς Ῥήγιον,
καὶ μετὰ μίαν ἡμέραν ἐπιγενομένου νότου δευτεραῖοι
ἤλθομεν εἰς Ποτιόλους, 14 οὗ εὑρόντες ἀδελφοὺς παρε-

κλήθημεν παρ' αὐτοῖς ἐπιμεῖναι ἡμέρας ἑπτά· καὶ οὕτως
εἰς τὴν Ῥώμην ἤλθαμεν 15 κἀκεῖθεν οἱ ἀδελφοὶ ἀκούσαντες
τὰ περὶ ἡμῶν ἦλθαν εἰς ἀπάντησιν ἡμῖν ἄχρι Ἀππίου
Φόρου καὶ Τριῶν Ταβερνῶν, οὓς ἰδὼν ὁ Παῦλος εὐχαρι-
στήσας τῷ θεῷ ἔλαβεν θάρσος. 16 ὅτε δὲ εἰσήλθομεν εἰς
Ῥώμην, ἐπετράπη τῷ Παύλῳ μένειν καθ' ἑαυτὸν σὺν τῷ
φυλάσσοντι αὐτὸν στρατιώτῃ.

No one who surveys these passages can any longer uphold the position that the author of the Acts has here *edited* and *incorporated* in his work an original document which had come into his hands. Why is this hypothesis excluded? Not only because of the general impression made by the overpowering multitude of coincidences, but above all because of two indications whose evidence is complementary:—(1) *In no other part of the Acts of the Apostles are the peculiarities of vocabulary and style of the author of the twofold work so accumulated and concentrated as they are in the "we"-sections.* I have thoroughly investigated both halves of the history as to vocabulary and style from all imaginable points of view and in all possible combinations, and I can answer for the statement—which is, moreover, suggested by a glance at the foregoing text, with its underlined passages—that Luke, *i.e.* the author of the twofold historical work, proves himself as an author to be nowhere more Lukan than in the "we"-sections. Setting aside the technicalities of the chapter on the shipwreck, very many more singularities of style are to be found in any other part of the Acts and the gospel of St Luke than in the "we"-sections.

These sections, however, both in vocabulary and style, bring the author complete in himself before our eyes; here, as in a jewel case, the critic of language and style finds heaped together all that goes to make the peculiar character of this author; while the other passages of the book may be said to have only a share, though it be an important share, in the treasure. This is just what we should expect upon the hypothesis of the identity of the author of the "we"-sections and of the author of the whole work (while upon the contrary hypothesis it presents an insoluble problem); for in the "we"-sections *alone* he writes quite independently, because he simply reports his own experiences; while in all the rest of the work he is dependent upon oral and written tradition, which has so influenced his vocabulary and style that, as we have already mentioned above, in the portions derived from Q scarcely 3 of the 261 words peculiar to St Luke make their appearance (to say nothing of the Semitic syntax in which these passages are composed).[1] Nearest in style to the "we"-sections come parts of the second half of the Acts in which the "we" does not occur. This, again, is just what we should have expected; for here the author certainly had no *written* sources at his disposal and no *fixed* oral tradition to depend upon, and could thus let himself go.—(2) "*Lukanisms,*" *if I may use the word, are as strongly represented in the fundamental passages, those which express the aim and interests of the "we"-sections, as in the subsidiary passages and all that belongs to the external literary form of these sections.* If we were only con-

[1] *Vide* my *Sayings of Jesus*, pp. 157 ff.

cerned with Lukanisms in the subsidiary passages it might be said that the author of the Acts had accidentally come into the possession of a record written by a man extraordinarily like himself in disposition and education. Such an accident, taking into account all the details of coincidence, would be strange enough, neither can I think of an instance comparable with it. Still, it is just possible that, among certain circles of the cultured middle class, agreement in vocabulary and modes of expression had become extraordinarily close; somewhat in the same way as among our newspaper circles of to-day a reporting style of meagre sameness has been evolved. But this is not the only phenomenon that presents itself to our notice. It is not only in the literary form in which the author of the Acts expresses what interests him, but also in his sphere of interest itself, that he shows himself identical with the author of the "we"-sections. Only on the hypothesis of a thorough, nay, an absolutely revolutionary, editing of the source on the part of the author of the complete work does this phenomenon become in any sense intelligible; as, indeed, is also admitted by the few critics who have gone into the question at all thoroughly;[1]

[1] *Vide* Schürer (*Theol. Lit. Ztg.*, 1906, col. 405, in his notice of my *Luke the Physician*): "All the statistical facts brought forward by Harnack are quite satisfactorily explained on the two hypotheses that (1) the author of the 'we'-source and the author of the Acts belong to the same sphere of culture and linguistic expression, and that (2) the latter did not incorporate his source unaltered, but revised its language." But why in the world should he have so severely edited a simple, straightforward record of events whose style was similar in character to his own? The example to which Schürer refers, the revision of Q (also

the hypothesis of an accidental likeness between the two authors as authors is in this case insufficient. If, however, we try the hypothesis of revision, *every possibility of ascertaining what really stood in the source at once vanishes*; for the "revision" must have been so detailed and so severe that it is now simply impossible to form any distinct conception of the source. And yet in spite of this we are to suppose that the "we" was carefully preserved while everything else was recast!

Let us take, by way of trial, the account of the shipwreck! If a source were present here it would be exceedingly improbable *a priori* that we should discover between it and the rest of the Acts of the Apostles or the gospel of St Luke any relationship either in language or in style that would be worthy of mention; for neither work is elsewhere concerned with sea voyages. And yet, how overwhelming even here is the multitude of coincidences! *Let us consider only the first three verses.*

Verse 1. ὡς δέ] is specifically Lukan; it is nowhere found in St Mark and St Matthew, in St Luke (Gospel and Acts) on the other hand it is exceedingly frequent, and that in all parts of both works.—ἐκρίθη] κρίνειν does not occur in this weakened sense in St Matthew, St Mark, and St John, nor is it found at all frequently in this significance; yet St Luke uses it thus no less than twelve times.—τοῦ ἀποπλεῖν ἡμᾶς εἰς τὴν Ἰταλίαν] Compare with this not very common construction

of St Mark) in the third gospel, is not a parallel instance; for these sources were written in a style which the cultured editor could not allow to remain unaltered.

Acts xxiii. 15: ἕτοιμοί ἐσμεν τοῦ ἀνελεῖν αὐτόν, also St Luke iv. 10: ἐντελεῖται τοῦ διαφυλάξαι σε.[1]—ἀποπλεῖν in the New Testament is exclusively Lukan, *vide* Acts xiii. 4; xiv. 26; xx. 15.—ἀποπλεῖν εἰς as in Acts xiii. 4 and xiv. 26.—Ἰταλίαν for Ῥώμην as Acts xviii. 2.—παρεδίδουν] The use of the imperfect here is peculiar; it is perhaps intended to express that the ship came from elsewhere, hence St Paul and the other prisoners embarked while the ship was on her voyage (*vide* Blass on this verse). The delicate use of the imperfect is not rare with St Luke, and is worthy of special investigation. In the "we"-sections alone are found 40–50 imperfects (apart from imperfect participles).—τόν τε Παῦλον καί τινας ἑτέρους δεσμώτας] ἕτερος is a word of which St Luke is particularly fond: it is found 51 times in his writings (never in St Mark, once in St John). In combination with τις it is also found in Acts viii. 34: ἑαυτοῦ ἢ περὶ ἑτέρου τινός.—ἑκατοντάρχῃ ὀνόματι Ἰουλίῳ σπείρης Σεβαστῆς] Other passages testify to St Luke's fondness for introducing numerous subordinate personages by name, and that *just in this way; vide* St Luke i. 5; v. 27; x. 38; xvi. 20; xix. 2; xxiii. 50;

[1] Moulton (*Grammar*,[3] 1908, p. 218) remarks concerning τοῦ *c. inf.*: "Luke supplies two-thirds of the total for the New Testament. In Luke we have 23 exx., of which five may be due to dependence on a noun, and about one-half seem clearly final; in Acts there are twenty-one with two adnominal and less than half final. . . . Before turning to grammatical detail let us parenthetically commend the statistics just given to the ingenious analysts who reject the unity of the Lucan books. The uniformity of use is very marked throughout Luke and Acts: *cf.* Acts xxvii. 1 ('we'-document) with xv. 20; xx. 3; Luke xxi. 22 with Acts ix. 15; xx. 27 ('we'-document) with xiv. 18."

Acts v. 1, 34; viii. 9; ix. 10, 11, 12, 33, 36; x. 1; xi. 28; xii. 13; xvi. 1, 14; xvii. 34; xviii. 2, 7, 24; xix. 24; xx. 9; xxi. 10; xxviii. 7, where ὀνόματι is found in each case. Again he here expressly adds the name of the σπεῖρα. We may compare Acts x. 12: ἀνήρ τις ὀνόματι Κορνήλιος ἑκατοντάρχης ἐκ σπείρης τῆς καλουμένης Ἰταλικῆς. Except in these two passages the name of a σπεῖρα is not found in the whole New Testament, and how similar is the construction of the two clauses!

Verse 2. ἐπιβάντες δὲ πλοίῳ Ἀδραμυττηνῷ] ἐπιβαίνω is, with the exception of the quotation from the LXX. in St Matt. xxi. 5, absolutely peculiar to the Acts, *vide* xx. 18; xxi. 2, 4; xxv. 1. In the last passage, as here, it occurs with the dative. The interest which is shown even in such details as the name of a ship is not peculiar to the "we"-sections, but appears also in other parts of the book if St Luke was in the position to satisfy it: *vide* my *Acts of the Apostles*, pp. 49 ff.—μέλλοντι πλεῖν εἰς τοὺς κατὰ τὴν Ἀσίαν τόπους] The use of μέλλειν (*vide* Moulton under this heading) is especially frequent with St Luke (47 times, twice in St Mark); μέλλειν ἔσεσθαι, which is found in the "we"-account xxvii. 10, is found again in the New Testament only in Acts xi. 28 and xxiv. 15!—The *simplex* πλεῖν is found once in the "we"-sections, elsewhere in the New Testament only in St Luke viii. 23 and Rev. xviii. 17.—The expression εἰς τ. κατὰ τ. Ἀσίαν τόπους is specifically Lukan: *vide* for τόπους Acts xvi. 3: τοὺς Ἰουδαίους τοὺς ὄντας ἐν τοῖς τόποις ἐκείνοις, for κατὰ τ. Ἀσίαν Acts xi. 1: οἱ ὄντες κατὰ τὴν Ἰουδαίαν, for Ἀσία in the sense of the Roman province (so everywhere in this book) see my *Acts of the Apostles*, p. 91 f.

ἀνήχθημεν] The word is wanting in St Mark and St John, it occurs once in both St Matthew and St Paul, while in St Luke's writings it is found 21 times. It is used of a ship not only in the "we"-account but also in St Luke viii. 22; Acts xiii. 13; xviii. 21.

ὄντος σὺν ἡμῖν Ἀριστάρχου Μακεδόνος Θεσσαλονικέως] *vide* xxii. 9: *οἱ σὺν ἐμοὶ ὄντες* and other passages. Σύν is, as is well known, a rare preposition in St Matthew, St Mark, and St John; in all three together it is found only 10 times (in Q not at all); in the Lukan writings, however, 77 times.—It is characteristic of St Luke to combine city and province, *i.e.* to be careful to give the name of the province together with the city; *vide* my *Acts of the Apostles*, pp. 59 ff. Twice, indeed, he writes Ταρσεὺς (Ταρσὸς) τῆς Κιλικίας (xxi. 39; xxii. 3). This is more remarkable than the present passage, because in it Μακεδόνος comes first.

Verse 3. *τῇ τε ἑτέρᾳ κατήχθημεν εἰς Σιδῶνα*] This use of *τε* for the continuation of the narrative, though not to be found in St Matthew, St Mark, and St Luke, occurs in Acts i. 15; ii. 33, 37, 40; iv. 13, 14, 33; v. 19; xiii. 52; and in very many other passages.—*τῇ ἑτέρᾳ* occurs here only; for in xx. 15 it is most probable that *ἑσπέρᾳ* should be read, a word found in the New Testament only in the "we"-sections, in the Acts (iv. 3; xxviii. 23), and in the gospel of St Luke (xxiv. 29).—*κατάγειν* is found with St Luke (gospel and Acts) 8 times, elsewhere in the New Testament only once (Rom. x. 6: τὸν Χριστὸν καταγαγεῖν). Also in St Luke v. 11 it is used of a ship (καταγαγόντες τὰ πλοῖα).

φιλανθρώπως τε ὁ Ἰούλιος τῷ Παύλῳ χρησάμενος ἐπέτρεψεν] This is the only clause in the first three verses of chap. xxvii. which, apart from the use of τε as a connective in the narrative, has no lexical nor stylistic kinship with the rest of the text of St Luke.

πρὸς τοὺς φίλους πορευθέντι ἐπιμελείας τυχεῖν] Πορεύεσθαι is a very favourite word with St Luke (88 times; in St Mark it is wanting altogether, in St Matthew it is not rare); notice also the Lukan participle. For φίλους, *vide* xix. 21; x. 34.—ἐπιμέλεια only here in the New Testament, but it is with St Luke alone that we find ἐπιμελεῖσθαι (St Luke x. 34 f.) and ἐπιμελῶς (St Luke xv. 8).—τυγχάνειν is wanting in St Matthew, St Mark, and St John; see however St Luke xx. 35: τοῦ αἰῶνος ἐκείνου τυχεῖν, Acts xxiv. 3: πολλῆς εἰρήνης τυγχάνοντες, Acts xxvi. 22: ἐπικουρίας τυχών. In the "we"-section xxviii. 2 we read: οὐ τὴν τυχοῦσαν φιλανθρωπίαν, and in Acts xix. 11: δυνάμεις οὐ τὰς τυχούσας ἐποίει ὁ θεός.

All these coincidences are found in the small compass of three verses! That this is due to accident, and that through accident the author of the Acts had come into the possession of an original document whose style and vocabulary so completely, and in every tiny detail, coincided with his own, is an impossible assumption. Hence, if one would escape from the admission of identity, there remains only the hypothesis that the author has entirely recast the document that had come into his hands. But what were the words of this document, and what could have led the editor to recast a record so absolutely simple in character? No! everyone must recognise that we have here primary narrative, that there has been here no working up nor revision. Thus the author of the "we"-account, and the author of the Acts of the Apostles who writes in exactly the same style as he, are one and the same person. What we have been able to demonstrate from these three verses can be also shown in all that follows. Of course, we must not make absurd demands and expect to find the technical terms of the "Shipwreck" in the sayings of our Lord, or in the narrative of His life, or in the stories concerning the early community in Jerusalem. But wherever a passage in the "we"-account at all admits of comparison, parallels with the Acts and the Lukan gospel at once make their appearance; *indeed, as the text above printed shows, there are only few verses even in the story of the Shipwreck which do not contain one or more parallels!* Among these are such striking instances as verses 34, 35. However, still more impressive than the coincidences in vocabulary are the coincidences in delicate characteristics of style which pervade the whole of these sections; in fact, *in the "we"-sections the author speaks his own language and writes in his usual style;*[1] *in the rest of the work just so much of this style makes its appearance as was allowed by the nature of the sources*

[1] It is therefore not surprising that he here shows himself a more cultivated and refined writer than in the rest of the work where either the style of the Septuagint is purposely imitated or the sources are allowed to preserve their characteristics.

which he used and the historical and religious colouring which he aimed at imparting.

One of the weightiest arguments for the identity of the author of the "we"-sections with the author of the twofold work, that is, for its composition by the physician St Luke, is the demonstration of the author's knowledge of and interest in matters of medicine. The instances produced first of all by Hobart, and then by Zahn and myself, have been assailed by P. W. Schmidt[1] and Clemen.[2] The former seeks to deprive a part of them of their force, in some cases perhaps with success; and yet he himself allows (S. 16 f.) that: "A good acquaintance with medical science and terminology may be ascribed to 'Luke.'"[3] This is quite enough for my purpose. One of a sceptical turn of mind may with reason dispute that the author of the Acts was a practising physician. If he, however, admits that this author possessed a good acquaintance with medical science and terminology, then the unanimous tradition that the author was Luke the physician receives the strongest support; for to what other Christian writer of the first two centuries can we ascribe such good acquaintance? To none that I know of. Certainly *it is possible* that even a layman—Schmidt lays stress upon this point—could have been interested in medical matters and have possessed good medical

[1] *Loc. cit.*, S. 6-18.

[2] *Loc. cit.*, pp. 785 ff.

[3] Schmidt describes this as the most that can be said in this connection.

information; but is it permissible to assume a well-informed layman of this kind, when tradition with all explicitness names a physician? That would indeed be a rare freak of chance! Clemen makes even further admissions. In set terms he allows: "that the author of the 'we'-sections was a physician can be regarded as probable." When, however, he continues, "but that such a one was the compiler of the whole book of Acts and of the third gospel, is very improbable," he has not considered that those very instances which speak in favour of the medical interest and information of the author are more weakly represented in the "we"-sections than in the rest of the work. If the author of the "we"-sections is a physician, then much more is the author of the whole twofold work; both, indeed, are physicians, because they are only a single person. Hence, even taking together the half admissions of these two scholars, it follows that the *autor ad Theophilum* was a physician, and that the tradition is therefore justified. In conclusion, among other objections I have heard it said that one does not even know that St Luke was a physician; some would have him to have been a painter. I refrain from refuting this argument; for it sets the record of St Paul, the contemporary and friend of St Luke, on a line with an obscure Byzantine legend.

I must, however, touch upon a very unmethodical and—I cannot describe it otherwise—thoughtless objection of Clemen. He writes (p. 786) that I have started from false premises, since in dealing with the "we"-source I have confined myself to those sections in which the "we" occurs, while from the way in which these sections make their entrance and exit in the book we can conclude with certainty that the source must have been more comprehensive and must also have included verses in which the "we" does not occur; "so one of the two objects Harnack compares with each other is to be circumscribed otherwise." It is a matter of controversy whether the "we"-sections form a source at all; it is, however, a still more disputable question, or rather a question involved in hopeless obscurity, how far this source, if there were such a source, extends. It is a matter of common knowledge that some scholars, in spite of the absence of the "we," include in it almost the whole second half of the Acts. But how can a man, who does not believe in the source at all, extend its boundary beyond the occurrence of the "we"? This would be a more difficult task for him than the squaring of the circle! Neither can he attach himself to any hypothesis, which has gained a fair amount of acceptance, concerning the extent of the supposed source, seeing that no such hypothesis exists.[1] Hence it

[1] Compare the guesses of Overbeck, Pfleiderer, v. Soden, Clemen, and many others concerning the extent of the supposed "we"-source, and note how widely they differ. P. W. Schmidt himself is not in agreement with Overbeck's idea of the source, and confines it within much more modest bounds (S. 46). He too repeats the assertion that the abrupt character of the entrance of the "we" proves that a source here makes its appearance (S. 45). But the question really stands thus: the absolute abruptness of the entrance and exit of the ἡμεῖς is in any case a strange and perplexing fact (yet in xvi. 10, on closer consideration, the entrance is not altogether abrupt). But it is not to be seen why it is less objectionable to suppose that upon each occasion some source makes its appearance than to suppose that the author who was present at the given time abruptly introduces himself as an eyewitness.

was not only correct in method, but also the only possible course, to bring together only those passages where the "we" actually occurs. All else that could be done I have already done, seeing that, in my investigation of the vocabulary of the "we"-sections in relation to the whole work, I have distinguished between the first and second halves of the Acts; *vide Luke the Physician*, pp. 67 ff. Clemen ought to have noticed this. He would then also have seen that the relation of the "we"-source to the first half of the work is not essentially different from its relation to the second half; so that even if we extend the source considerably beyond the limits of the actual "we"-sections, the close relationship with the whole work and with the gospel of St Luke remains unaffected. Just as, in the investigation of Q, I confined myself strictly to those passages which, apart from Markan sections, are common to St Matthew and St Luke, because otherwise all certainty vanishes,[1] so also in dealing with the

The former hypothesis is to me much more doubtful and objectionable, especially when one must assume that the author has thoroughly revised the source and yet has allowed the "we" to remain. In this case, indeed, it is difficult to suppress a suspicion of intentional deception. Schmidt, it is true, will have nothing to do with an hypothesis of editorial transformation (S. 46: "apart from perhaps one sentence, xxviii. 8, no evidence can be adduced that Luke has anywhere [! !] exercised even a modifying influence upon the 'we'-sections"); in forming such an opinion he cannot have realised the force of the argument from language and style.

[1] But even for this I have been found fault with by those critics among whom there is slight recognition of the fact that in these matters the first consideration of all is to find firm foothold and to produce real evidence instead of working in a fog of uncertainties. Such critics, however, are, I am sorry to say, in the majority.

supposed "we"-source I am compelled to confine myself strictly to the "we." The difference consists only in this, that both in St Matthew and St Luke there are certainly other sections which come from Q (only they cannot be distinguished with certainty), while the "we"-source cannot have contained more than the "we"-sections, because it is nothing but a phantom.

The most plausible argument for the distinction of the "we"-sections from the complete work is, after all, that tone, that *nuance* of historical sobriety and actuality, which distinguishes these sections more especially from the first half of the book.[1] All that can be advanced in this connection has been collected together in my *Acts of the Apostles*, chap. iv. pp. 133 ff., 141 ff., and 144 ff. But I have there also shown that a criticism of this kind applies to those parts of the second half of the Acts, in which the "we" is wanting, with much more force than to the "we"-sections. I can therefore only repeat what I have already stated summarily at p. 143 of the work just mentioned: St Luke—whose own "we"-account shows him to have been a physician endowed with miraculous gifts—possessed for the first half of the Acts a source, or sources (oral or written), which was congenial to his own peculiar temperament—indeed, in this direction went even further than himself.

[1] One might also add the *nuance* of meagreness and brevity which distinguishes them from the other passages of the last third of the book, were not the "shipwreck" dealt with in such striking fulness. The long, and to a great extent identical, speeches of the last quarter of the book must proceed from some purpose of the author which we cannot fathom quite satisfactorily.

On the other hand, for the second half he did not possess such sources (with the exception of what is told us of Ephesus), but only, so far as he was not himself an eyewitness, had at his disposal simple records, into which he has inserted nothing except two conventional accounts of visions (xviii. 8 ff.; xxiii. 10 ff.), which illustrate the development of the plot. It cannot be otherwise; for if he himself had introduced the supernatural element into chapters i.–xv., it is unintelligible why he should have refrained from doing the same thing in the second half, except, or almost only except, where he himself was an eyewitness. That the parts of the narrative where the colouring is most sober are not the "we"-sections, but the accounts of St Paul's visits to Thessalonica, Berœa, Athens, Corinth, Jerusalem (the last visit), Cæsarea, and Rome, is a convincing proof that his narrative is kept in close accordance with sources of information. The crasser traits in the first half of the work (*vide* pp. 144 ff.) are explained by the crasser calibre of the sources. An historian, however, who clearly enough wishes us to regard the story of Eutychus as an instance of resurrection from the dead, and the story of St Paul and the serpent likewise as a miracle (and yet in either case shrinks from tampering with the facts themselves), who, moreover, represents the Apostle in the Shipwreck as prophet in the popular sense—such an one could very well, indeed with special pleasure, relate crass things such as those we read in the first half of the Acts. We ought not, of course, to overlook the difference in the miraculous accounts as given in the "we"-sections and the first half of the book; still less, however, ought we to forget the strong agreement wherein they are bound together; see above all, chap. xxvii. 22–26.

The gulf which divides the author of the "we"-accounts from the author of the whole Acts of the Apostles, is not wider than the gulf which yawns between Eusebius the chronicler of the first books of the *Ecclesiastical History* and Eusebius the sober-minded historian; it is in my opinion considerably less wide, and yet the ultimate ground for reluctance in recognising the unity of the Acts and the "we"-account is to be found in the gulf which yawns between the first chapters of the work and the "we"-account—a gulf which it is thought cannot be bridged over. I can only repeat that the gulf that lies between chaps. xvi.–xxviii., *minus the "we"-sections*, and chaps. i.–v. is considerably wider. The elasticity and play of feeling which we recognise and do not regard as out of place, not only in such authors as Eusebius and Sulpicius Severus, but even in a Livy and Tacitus, we must also allow to such an one as St Luke. Baur's criticism has brought us much that is valuable, but it has not escaped the danger of making the writers of the New Testament, one and all, merely *types*, with the consequence that a less rigid view must appear as wanting in logical accuracy, if not as something worse. As a result, either the authors were driven into exile out of their own period, or their works were condemned to amputation and mutilation. This danger has in essential points been removed through the advance of science; yet there still remains a disposition to conceive of a writer of the New Testament as more of a type and to make more stringent demands upon his consistency—and even upon his conscientiousness, inward integrity, and intellectual constancy — than human nature can bear, and than the spirit and circumstances of the times allowed.

The unanimous tradition that St Luke is the author of the Acts of the Apostles has come to us with the book itself.[1] Besides the acquaintance which the author of the third gospel and the Acts shows with medical subjects, this tradition is supported by the following considerations, which I have developed in greater detail elsewhere (*Luke the Physician*, pp. 12 ff.).

1. St Luke is nowhere mentioned by name in the Acts, which is just what we should expect if he himself were the author of the book. On the other hand, Aristarchus, who appears in the Epistles of St Paul side by side with St Luke, is thrice mentioned by name. Why is St Luke left out?[2] For one who is assured of the Lukan authorship the answer is very simple, for one who opposes that view it is not an altogether easy one.

2. St Luke was, according to St Paul, a *Greek*, belonging to the middle plane of culture; so was the author of this great historical work.

[1] Even if the tradition were false, it could not have arisen later than the beginning of the second century, and then only through *correction* of the original title; for, as the dedication shows, the work was not anonymous. This consideration makes it difficult to believe that the title κατὰ Λουκᾶν is mistaken.

[2] The omission of Titus—who is the only other person we should expect to find mentioned in the Acts—is not so strange, because he is not elsewhere mentioned with St Luke. Moreover, Titus was not in such an independent position as St Luke in relation to St Paul.

3. St Luke, according to St Paul's epistles, was at times the Apostle's companion; so was the author of the Acts, and *both* were with St Paul in Rome, whither he came with only two companions. Again, judging from the Pauline epistles, it is improbable that St Luke was with St Paul when he wrote the epistles to the Thessalonians, the Corinthians, and the Romans. From the Acts we deduce that the author was not *at that time* in the Apostle's company.

4. The author of the third gospel was acquainted with the gospel of St Mark; we know from the Pauline epistles that St Luke and St Mark were sometimes together (wherever in the Pauline epistles St Luke's name is found, there also we find the name of St Mark). The author of the Acts actually knows the name of a maid-servant in St Mark's house.

5. St Luke, according to the testimony of St Paul, was not only his companion but also his "fellow-worker" (thus not simply a serving brother, like Timothy). From the Acts we deduce (xvi. 10, 13) that its author was an active missionary, working together with St Paul in a position of some independence.

6. St Luke, according to good tradition, belonged to an Antiochian family; the author of the Acts of the Apostles, as appears from his work, stood in an especially close relationship with Antioch, and most probably made use of a source which had its origin in that city.—Of these arguments only a few refer to the "we"-sections alone.

CHAPTER II

THE CHIEF ARGUMENT AGAINST THE LUKAN AUTHORSHIP OF THE ACTS: JEWISH CHRISTIANITY (JUDAISM), ST PAUL AND ST LUKE

THE following are the principal arguments that are generally adduced against the composition of the Acts by St Luke:—

1. Numerous discrepancies and blunders in historical details, such as cannot be ascribed to a companion of St Paul, even if he were only at times in the company of the Apostle.

2. The representation of the Council of Jerusalem and of the Apostolic Decree (contrast Gal. ii.).

3. The portraiture of St Paul, unsatisfactory in general and incorrect in particular, in so far as it assigns to the Apostle an attitude towards Jewish Christianity (Judaism) which is inconsistent with that of his epistles.

Of these arguments I have thoroughly investigated the first partly in my first study, *Luke the Physician*, partly in my *Acts of the Apostles*, pp. 203 ff., and I hope that it may pass as refuted. I have shown that St Luke, with all his general excellence as an historian, was careless and negligent in details of narrative, and has thus to answer for many discrepancies of smaller or greater importance. The real mistakes, however, never go so far as to make it no longer possible to maintain that the writer was an occasional companion of St Paul. We must assume that only, or almost only, in those parts of his work where the "we" occurs was St Luke an eyewitness of what he records, so that in all the rest of his narrative he was dependent upon written or oral information. The mere employment of these sources would produce discrepancies — even in the second half of the work,—abbreviations of the narrative leading to obscurity, and so forth, which are the less remarkable seeing that they are not wanting even in the "we"-sections. However, these mistakes, which are for the most part harmless, even though they are often gross blunders, do not as a whole avail to alter our judgment concerning the value of the narrative and concerning the personality of the historian; even though we must deplore that he had not at his disposal better authorities for the first half of his work, that his plan excluded very many things about which we should gladly have been informed, and that he loves nothing better than to tell the wonders of Christian Science.

As for the second argument, it has been dealt with in detail in *Acts of the Apostles*, pp. 248–263. Together with Hilgenfeld and Resch jun., I endeavoured to show that the authorities of the Western Text present the original version of the Apostolic Decree, and that, if this is true, the historical difficulty, which this decree has hitherto presented, now vanishes.

My exposition has met with only slight approval;[1] but I cannot see that it has been disproved. The interpretation of the decree, as if it were concerned with regulations about meats, makes shipwreck upon the simple fact that St Luke, in Acts xv., puts into the mouth of no less an one than St James the words that "Moses" need not be imposed upon the Gentile Christians, seeing that he had continually his *observatores* among the circumcised. "Moses" surely implies laws concerning meats. Again, the imposition of laws concerning meats would then only have significance if it were a question of establishing communion and fellowship between Jewish and Gentile Christians. But nothing is said of this either in Acts xv. or Gal. ii. The point in controversy was simply the recognition of the principle of a mission to the Gentiles without the imposition of the yoke of the Law upon the converted. To receive this recognition it was necessary that the Gentile Christians should observe the fundamental laws of morality. But I cannot here repeat all that I wrote three years ago. However, even supposing that I was mistaken, there

[1] Schürer (*Theol. Lit. Ztg.*, 1908, col. 175), P. W. Schmidt (*loc. cit.*, S. 18 ff.), Clemen (*loc. cit.*, pp. 794 ff.), Sanday, Bacon, Diehl, Bousset, etc., have declared against me. I imagine that I have shown (*Acts of the Apostles*, pp. 248 ff.) that the Apostolic Decree alone here stands in question (the rest of the description of the Apostolic Council in Acts xv., be its mistakes many or few, could very well have proceeded from a later companion of St Paul). On this point many scholars who find the decree itself a stumbling-block are at one with me. Finally, the Apostolic Epistle is also not in question. Even Blass admits that in it St Luke himself has summarised the chief points, a procedure which was open to the historian of antiquity.

arises, it is true, a certain doubt as to St Luke's authorship; but a negative decision, in face of all the evidence that speaks *for* St Luke, as well as in itself, is altogether too precipitate. In the first place, it must be remembered that the words of Acts xv. 28 (μηδὲν πλέον ἐπιτίθεσθαι ὑμῖν βάρος πλὴν τούτων τῶν ἐπάναγκες) presuppose that those addressed were already bearing this burden. Next, I refer on the one hand to Zahn, *Einleitung*, ii., S. 437 ff., whose remarks concerning the scope of the decree in its Western form (which he regards as original) deserve all consideration, and, on the other hand, to what I myself have written in answer to Schürer (*Theol. Lit. Ztg.*, 1906, col. 467). (1) Concerning the *more intimate* relationship of St Luke with St Paul in theological views, nothing is known to us; we only know that he makes his appearance in St Paul's company as from the first a relatively *independent* evangelist. To what extent he shared St Paul's peculiar views can be learned only from his own works. The common assumption that a companion of St Paul must be pictured simply according to the pattern of the master is without any basis, and is doubly reprehensible in the case of a Gentile of no slight culture, who already, before his conversion to Christianity, was in touch with the Synagogue. Tatian was a disciple of Justin, and mentions Justin with the highest praise in the very work which shows us how far in teaching he is removed from his master. (2) When St Luke wrote, the ecclesiastical situation was different from what it was at the time of the Apostolic Council and the Epistle to the Galatians. (3) We have no means of knowing what kind of reports other than information derived from St Paul, St Luke possessed concerning the Council, nor what was the bias of his authorities. St Luke in all probability described that event just as ancient historians again and again describe controversies of the past—that is, from the standpoint of their own times. What he puts into the mouth of St Peter and St James is in part at least very appropriate; but there is absolutely no reason why the author, even though a companion of St Paul, should not have invented it. He did not, at all events, invent the central fact that the leaders on both sides came to an agreement that was temporarily satisfactory, and that the mission to the Gentiles was thus recognised; for here we have also the testimony of the Epistle to the Galatians. Acts xv. is not to be regarded as a protocol nor is the Epistle to the Galatians; indeed, the account given in this epistle, written in all the agitation of soul of an insulted apostle and an injured father, and glowing with passionate indignation, not against the Primitive Apostles but against those who were disturbing the peace of the Galatian church, is anything rather than a perfect record; and, in spite of its complete trustworthiness in main points, it gives absolutely no description of the course of the conferences which led up to the verdict, and offers no guarantee that important circumstances of secondary rank have not been left unmentioned. Without in the least degree impeaching the integrity of the Apostle, one may also ask whether the relation of rank in which St Paul stood to the Primitive Apostles, as actually expressed in the negotiations of the Council, was quite what St Paul himself regards it in Gal. i. 1 ff. He himself writes in chap. ii. 2: μή πως εἰς κενὸν τρέχω ἢ ἔδραμον. P. W. Schmidt (*loc. cit.*, S. 26), indeed, in his anxiety lest St Paul the hero and the saint should suffer detriment in a single trait of his character, cries: "Where else in the epistles has an emotion snatched the reins from the hand of St Paul!" In the face of not a few passages of the Pauline epistles I cannot join in this exclamation.

But to very many scholars the third seems to be the decisive argument against the composition of the Acts by St Luke. Just as in days gone by, Baur, Hausrath, and others advanced it with the strongest emphasis ("it is more credible that Calvin on his death-bed should have vowed a golden dress to the Mother of God than that St Paul should have acted in this fashion"), so now it is thrust forward as the greatest obstacle to be surmounted. Thus Schürer (*Lit. Ztg.*, 1906, col. 408) writes: "No companion of St Paul could have put into the Apostle's mouth the statement that he was accused because of the hope of the Resurrection (xxiii. 6), or because of the hope of the promise given to the fathers (xxvi. 6); the companion of St Paul (who wrote the "we"-account) knew that the reason of the imprisonment was quite different." Again (*loc. cit.*, 1908, col. 176): "Can we really believe that a well-informed companion of St Paul could have put into his mouth the *gross untruth* of chaps. xxiii. 6 and xxvi. 6? From the more accurate report of xxi. 27 ff., we know that the reasons were quite otherwise." P. W.

Schmidt is still more pronounced. He rejects the narratives of the circumcision of Timothy, of the vows which, according to the Acts, St Paul undertook, etc.; he asserts with Overbeck that a "dogmatic Judaising" of St Paul pervades the Acts. Then he proceeds (S. 33): "In all important points Overbeck has pointed out the most obvious and surest way towards a purely scientific criticism of the Lukan work [what else does any of us wish for?]. On the other hand, in so far as the attempt of Harnack to enhance the historical reputation of the Acts is really successful, there inevitably follows a corresponding depreciation of the historical value of the Pauline epistles. *The only school of criticism which could rejoice in such a result of the investigation of the Lukan writings would be the school that would banish the Pauline epistles into the second century into the company of Marcion.*"

Similarly, but still more decidedly, writes Jülicher (*Neue Linien i. d. Kritik d. evangel. Überlief.*, 1906, S. 59 f.): "If the Acts of the Apostles is really correct in its portraiture of St Paul, if this colourless rhetorical representative of average Christianity is the genuine Paul, *then I can no longer resist the baleful attraction* [what attraction can there be?] *of the hypothesis proclaimed by the school of Leyden:* that Paul the great epistolary writer is a later fiction, an ideal form, which an unknown artist has elevated upon eagle's wings out of the lowly circumstances of the real Paul into heavenly heights. . . . Those, however, for whom the Paul of the four great epistles abides the most certain, the most unimpeachable thing in the whole New Testament, must describe the portraiture of St Paul in the Acts as woefully deficient and poor, just because it preserves absolutely nothing of the peculiar characteristics of the man: and if one who for many years was a companion, a friend, indeed a fellow-worker of St Paul—as was St Luke—in spite of the multitude of reminiscences which even in unimportant matters stood at his disposal, and in a writing where a picture of the genuine Paul was above all things called for—if such a one could not introduce into his portrait even *one* of the grand and noble characteristics of the Apostle, then indeed it is altogether vain to expect, or even to cherish a modest hope, that the Gospel historians, who depend entirely upon the testimony of others, present us with anything more than notices concerning external events in the life of our Lord and an artificial scheme of His ministry: how can we expect to receive from them genuine words from the lips of Jesus, or to feel through them the breath of His spirit pass upon us! If one of St Paul's most intimate friends tells us (Acts xxi. 20 ff.), without the slightest hesitation, that the Apostle when in Jerusalem was ready, merely for the sake of peace and *by a premeditated and elaborate act of hypocrisy*, to convince the Jews that he walked now as before in strict observance of the Law; and if this piece of information, alleged to be given by a *friend* who must have known St Paul's real attitude towards the Law, deserves to be described as good tradition, then all trust in an intelligent transmission of actual history in the Primitive Church sinks to nothing, and we can no longer oppose with confidence the negation even of the best-attested statements."

I could wish that Jülicher had not written these words; for while on the one hand they show a want of circumspection and accuracy of thought, and moreover introduce considerations that are alien to dispassionate judgment, on the other hand they are an echo of the criticism of Baur, Lipsius, and Hausrath, which in this point ought to be regarded as superseded. Seeing, however, that such distinguished scholars of the present day repeat the apprehensions which Lüdemann often expressed more than twenty years ago, when he asserted that my view of history (in my *History of Dogma*) led straight to the rejection of the genuineness of the Pauline epistles, it must be necessary to submit the point which gives rise to these apprehensions to a close examination. Of course, my opponents are as far as myself from allowing "consequences" to affect their recognition of the truth of any question, and this reference to "consequences" it were better to leave altogether out of consideration, because—apart from the shifting of standpoint that may easily be discovered in the argument—these consequences absolutely do not exist. Must the epistles of St Paul be spurious because he found in his companion St Luke a poor or, as far as my argument is concerned, even an untrustworthy biographer? What kind of logic is this? Where, however, St Paul himself, *rightly* interpreted from his own epistles, really stands opposed to St Luke—when have I ever given occasion to anyone to imagine that in such a case I should demand that the latter rather than the former ought to be believed? *But the real question is this, whether St Paul, on the point here in question—*

namely, his practical attitude towards Jewish Christianity and Judaism—has been rightly interpreted from his epistles by such scholars as Schürer, Jülicher, and P. W. Schmidt.[1] And next, in regard to the further question as to the character of St Luke as an historian, we are in the fortunate position of being able to compare his gospel with its sources St Mark and Q, and to ascertain the measure of freedom which he allows himself in their use; and from his two books we can moreover determine, with a great degree of certainty, his own views on Jewish Christianity and Judaism.[2]

[1] Schürer, moreover, took up an intermediate position. In the first place he held (in opposition to Jülicher) that Acts xxi. 27 ff. was a good and trustworthy account; secondly, he closed his review of my *Acts of the Apostles* (1908, col. 176) with the words: "More particularly I find myself at one with Harnack in the opinion that we arrive at a false impression of St Paul if we confine ourselves solely to the Epistle to the Galatians. The Apostle's own testimony in 1 Cor. ix. 20 is just as important. The perception of this point clears up many strange notices and stories in the Acts, though still only one class of the same." Other scholars also have expressed similarly moderate views. Wendt (*Comment. z. Ap. Gesch.*, S. 346 ff.), Pfleiderer (*Urchristentum*, I², S. 521 ff.), and Joh. Weiss (*Über Absicht. u. lit. Character der Ap. Gesch.*, S. 36 ff.) are of the opinion that Acts xxi. 23 ff. is practically correct, but that the reason for the action given in verse 24 is to be set to the account of the author of the Acts. Pfleiderer well remarks: "How far it is morally possible to proceed in 'accommodation' in matters that one regards as indifferent in themselves is a question that depends so much upon the particular case that it seems out of place to make any decision *a priori*. It is certain that St Paul regarded 'accommodation' for the sake of peace as right in principle." But was it only a question of "accommodation"? This concession does not go far enough, though it is far in advance of Jülicher, who is as convinced as the Asiatic and other Jews in Jerusalem that St Paul, if he took part in the Nazarite vow, was guilty of gross hypocrisy and deceit.

[2] Let me here, by the way, make the following remarks:—The difficulties in the way of the identification of the author of the Acts with

In determining to investigate the relations of St Paul with Jewish Christianity and Judaism I am aware that I am fixing my eye upon a point which is guarded by the critics with jealous care and with the whole ardour of Protestantism. The indignation into which they fall, not only if a statement of St Paul in the great epistles is not received with complete acquiescence, but even if *the absolute inward and outward consistency* of the Apostle is called in question, proves that they are convinced that they are defending a main fortress of their position. Though a situation of such a kind may not hinder a patient and scientific inquiry, it may well be detrimental to the persuasive power of the results of such an inquiry.

A.—St Paul's Attitude towards Jewish Christianity and Judaism according to his Epistles;[1] his Jewish Limitations

The problem with which we are here concerned is generally stated as follows: firstly, the description of the religious attitude of the Apostle to the Law, given

St Luke, a man who had companied with St Paul, are most strongly emphasised by the critics; but the difficulties that arise from supposing that the man who had spoken with Silas, James, Philip, and Mark nevertheless composed the third gospel, and the difficulty that St Mark the "interpreter" of St Peter should have written the second gospel, are relatively little noticed! According to my opinion, this is a case of straining out the gnat and swallowing the camel. *Vide infra* concerning the cause of this meting with two different measures.

[1] It is not proposed to give here a complete representation; attention will be drawn only to those points—though these are indeed the most important—which come under consideration in connection with the question of the faithfulness of the portrait drawn in the Acts.

in the epistle to the Galatians, is treated as a complete and absolute representation of St Paul's mind, and is regarded as the major premise; then as minor premise is added the saying: "To the Jews I became as a Jew, that I might gain Jews, although I myself am not under the law" (1 Cor. ix. 20). But the problem so stated, leading to the conclusion that St Paul continued to submit to Jewish customs *purely from motives of "accommodation,"* does not cover all the facts that come into view in connection with the attitude of the Apostle to Judaism and Jewish Christianity. The problem is more complicated.

It is certain—for we have also the testimony of the Epistles to the Romans and Corinthians—that the Apostle's religious attitude to the Law, as represented in the Epistle to the Galatians, was not a temporary position acquired, narrowly defined, and sharply formulated when he was engaged in a conflict of peculiar bitterness; it indeed formed a cardinal article of his profession of faith. St Paul never withdrew from the position that the Christian—that is, every Christian, Jew as well as Gentile—is no longer, from the religious standpoint, under the Law, *i.e.* the Law no longer comes into consideration so far as his relation to God and the *moral* value of his conduct are concerned; for as a child of God the Christian is led by the Spirit[1] which he has received; and the Law, in so far as righteousness was of the Law, is satisfied by Christ, "the end of the Law";

[1] In so far as the Christian has still a law to fulfil, it is the "law of Christ," the conditions of which are altogether different from the law of Moses; *vide* Grafe, *Die paulinische Lehre vom Gesetz*, 1884.

hence the Law is abolished. It further follows that in the sight of God and in their mutual relations and intercourse there can no longer be any distinction between Jew and Gentile. This is expressly stated not only in Gal. iii. 28, v. 6, but also in Rom. x. 12 and 1 Cor. vii. 19, xii. 13; and in these passages and elsewhere it is also said that they all are baptized *into one body* and are *all Abraham's children*, and that thus *the promises belong to them all.*

This position is so clear that it seems necessarily to exclude every doubt as to the proper attitude now to be adopted towards the Law and as to the attitude which St Paul himself adopted. Yet, as a matter of fact, we learn (1) from the accusations of his opponents, (2) from definite statements and arguments of the Apostle himself, that his attitude was different from what we should have expected.

1. As we may learn from the Epistle to the Galatians, the Judaising opponents of St Paul brought against him the accusation that he still[1] preached circumcision (v. 11), and that he thus stood in flagrant contradiction with himself. He must have given some occasion for such an accusation.[2]

2. Such occasions are to be found even in his epistles (not only in the story of Acts xvi. 3 that he had circumcised Timothy).

[1] To understand this "still" as if St Paul here admits that at the beginning of his missionary career he had still demanded circumcision, is quite uncalled for.

[2] In return the Apostle brings against his opponents the reproach (vi. 13) that they, while peremptorily demanding circumcision, did not themselves keep the Law.

(*a*) Here 1 Cor. vii. 18 f. above all comes into view. In this passage the Apostle gives to the circumcised the direction μὴ ἐπισπάσθω; for, says he, each should abide in the condition in which the Divine call found him. This μὴ ἐπισπάσθω, together with the general admonition, naturally cannot have only its narrow literal signification, nor can it only mean that the converted Jew should leave his children uncircumcised; it can only mean that the converted Jew should remain faithful to the customs and ordinances of the fathers. Though the motive is implicit it is nevertheless clear enough: that it has anything to do with salvation is most distinctly denied in verse 19 (ἡ περιτομὴ οὐδέν ἐστιν, καὶ ἡ ἀκροβυστία οὐδέν ἐστιν, ἀλλὰ τήρησις ἐντολῶν θεοῦ: *cf.* Gal. v. 6, where we read as the apodosis ἀλλὰ πίστις δι' ἀγάπης ἐνεργουμένη); the command, therefore, must have been given because St Paul recognised that it depended upon the Will of the Creator whether a man is born Jew or Gentile,[1] and because he felt that this Will ought to be respected. *This attitude in itself was enough to give rise to the charge that the Apostle taught circumcision, and this charge need not have been simply due to malice. Was it such a simple thing to distinguish between the saving Will of God and His Will as Creator, and to declare that according to the former Will the law was abrogated, while allowing it to stand for Jewish Christians according to the latter Will? Was one who attempted to draw such fine distinctions entirely above suspicion?*

(*b*) But in the Epistle to the Galatians itself this

[1] This is implied in the abbreviated expression ἐν τῇ κλήσει ᾗ ἐκλήθη.

opinion concerning the continuance of the obligation to observe the Law has received still harsher expression, so that it becomes at once explicable how the reproach of v. 11 could have been made. In Gal. v. 3, St Paul writes: "I testify again to every man that is circumcised that he is bound to observe the whole Law." This statement, according to St Paul's meaning, is by no means confined only to the circumcised who were not Christian, but applies also to circumcised Christians, otherwise it would not have been written in terms of such general connotation.[1] If we now add as a major premise that the Law no longer possesses religious and moral obligation because it has now absolutely ceased to exist as a divine means of salvation, we are again led to the same conclusion, that the Jewish Christian is to keep the Law because in it is given the manner of life which God had willed *for him.* Hence *the whole Law* continues to exist as custom and ordinance for Jewish Christians. *What a dialectic, to be sure, which allows God to preserve the Law in force as a customary rule of life for a particular circle of men, while asserting that the same God has abolished the Law as a means of attaining to righteousness, for all men, and thus also for those for whom it is still in force!* Can we then wonder that misunderstandings arose and that strong opposition was stirred up?

(*c*) But does St Paul, in asserting the lasting obligation upon Jewish Christians to observe the Law, really base his opinion solely upon the ground that the Jew still remains a Jew and therefore must con-

[1] So also B. Weiss, *Bibl. Theol.*, S. 348, and many other commentators.

tinue to live in accordance with Jewish custom and ordinance? Is this somewhat petty motive really the only one? By no means! The Epistle to the Romans here gives the needed information.

The great division formed by chaps. ix.-xi. of this epistle comes from the pen of one whose very soul is bound by every tie of passionate affection to his people. He is, to his most bitter sorrow, forced to recognise that this people, because of its unbelief, is on the way seemingly to eternal destruction. He struggles for light as to the purposes of God; he is ready himself to suffer eternal damnation if only his nation might be again accepted by God. Yet can the nation—*ὧν ἡ υἱοθεσία καὶ ἡ δόξα καὶ αἱ διαθῆκαι καὶ ἡ νομοθεσία καὶ ἡ λατρεία καὶ αἱ ἐπαγγελίαι, ὧν οἱ πατέρες καὶ ἐξ ὧν ὁ Χριστὸς τὸ κατὰ σάρκα*—actually come to destruction? What of the Divine promises and pledges? In chaps. ix. and x. the Apostle seems to acquiesce in the answer that the promises still remain in force because they apply to Israel *κατὰ πνεῦμα*. Through the gift of the righteousness which is by faith, the Gentile is engrafted into this Israel *κατὰ πνεῦμα*; and so this Israel continues to exist even if no Jew by birth is found therein! But this answer, though it ought to have sufficed, does not, nevertheless, satisfy the Apostle! Therefore in chap. xi. another entirely different view appears by the side of the first. *There is fulfilment of the Divine promises also for Israel κατὰ σάρκα.* God cannot and has not rejected His people—meaning here, Israel *κατὰ σάρκα*! As a proof there is: in the first place, the Apostle himself (verse 1: *καὶ γὰρ ἐγὼ Ἰσραηλείτης* εἰμί, ἐκ σπέρματος Ἀβραάμ, φυλῆς Βενιαμείν), together with those Jews, small though their number might be, who believed in Christ (verse 4);[1] and, secondly, there is the consideration that the present hardening and rejection of the Jews was intended—as the Apostle believed—to bring about that reception of the Gentiles into God's family which was now being accomplished. From this, he further concludes, it is certainly to be believed that the time of Israel κατὰ σάρκα will again come; for if it is possible to engraft twigs of the wild olive into the good olive, then still more must it be possible to engraft twigs that have been hewn off from the good olive into their own tree. Note that the (believing) Israel κατὰ σάρκα is and remains "the good olive tree" (in contrast with the wild olive tree of the Gentiles); every Israelite is a "natural branch" of this good olive tree even if he under circumstances must be hewn off; and the believing Israel κατὰ σάρκα is the root, in whose sap and fatness the engrafted wild shoots partake, and which bears them (verses 24, 17, 21, 18).[2] The sentence, "Uncircumcision is nothing and circumcision is nothing," has force only in reference to the

[1] Here we are reminded of Luther's answer to the anxious question of Melanchthon as to where the Church of Christ was now to be found. Would that the Apostle had abided by this view!

[2] Herzog very justly remarks in "Die Gefangennahme des Apostels Paulus," *Internat. Theol. Zeitschr.*, 1905, 5 Heft, S. 197 ff. (an article which belongs to the best that has been written about St Paul in the last years): "If St Peter or St James had used this simile of the olive tree it would without doubt have been regarded as a proof of the slight estimation in which the Jewish Apostles really held the Gentile Christians, and how very determined they were to make Christianity appear merely as a continuation of Judaism."

righteousness which is of faith; and there is a point of view from which it is not a matter of indifference whether a man is a Jew by birth or a Gentile. And St Paul now sums up with his philosophical reading of the great historical drama: "Hardening *ἀπὸ μέρους* hath befallen Israel [*κατὰ σάρκα*], until the fulness of the Gentiles be come in, and so *all* Israel [*κατὰ σάρκα*] shall be saved.[1] As touching the Gospel they are [God's] enemies for your sake [so that you Gentile Christians may now be engrafted], but as touching the election [before time began, which will be accomplished in the end of all things] they are [God's] beloved for the fathers' sake; for the gifts and the calling of God are without repentance."

There is no possibility of doubt—the Apostle teaches, so we may say, a double fulfilment of the promise, and he teaches that Israel *κατὰ πνεῦμα* is rooted and remains rooted in Israel *κατὰ σάρκα* in so far as it has become believing. The promise is fulfilled in that from people of all kinds—here there is no distinction between circumcision and uncircumcision—and by the free gift of the righteousness which is by faith, the *one* people of God is established. And yet, though this is indeed the chief part of the fulfilment, it is by no means the final, the perfect fulfilment. The fulfilment only

[1] *τὸ πλήρωμα τῶν ἐθνῶν* in regard to the number included has not the same significance as *πᾶς Ἰσραήλ*. The latter expression (compared with verse 7) means that in the fulness of the times the number of the rejected from Israel will be so small as not to count; the former expression leaves undecided the ratio of the Gentiles who are saved to the whole number, for the "plena copia" is determined by the *ἐκλογή* (verse 7).

becomes perfect when the pledges given to Israel *κατὰ σάρκα* are fulfilled, and *this* Israel, as was promised to the fathers, is saved, in order that thus Israel *κατὰ σάρκα*, even at the last, may hold its ground as the People of Promise.[1]

It is usual to admire the profundity of the philosophical interpretation of history upon which St Paul has based this hope of his, and our hearts are indeed moved with wonder and sympathy by his passionate devotion to his nation and its ancient customs and privileges; but we overlook, or out of respect to the greatness of the man do not dare to express, the fact that by this particular view his whole doctrine of faith is embarrassed, thrown into confusion, and rendered seriously inconsistent. Psychologically all is clear, and no single word of excuse is necessary; but practically this discordant addition (for so it may be described) which the Apostle makes to his doctrine of Salvation runs across the very principle of his faith and even counteracts its convincing force.[2] St Paul, *by an*

[1] B. Weiss (*loc. cit.*, S. 272) has correctly reproduced the thought of the Apostle: "While the privilege which was given to the nation of Israel through the Law could be turned into its opposite because of the sin of the nation, the privilege which the nation possessed in the promise of Messianic Salvation, because of its descent from the Patriarchs, was, and would continue to be, *inalienable*. . . . The free gifts of God, and especially the calling to the Messianic Salvation which had been granted to the *nation*, could not be repented of and could not be withdrawn." Compare also Rom. xv. 8; and Weiss justly remarks that, in spite of the actual revolution in the calling to the Salvation proclaimed in the Gospel, this Salvation, according to St Paul's view, was still, *in the first place*, for the Jews (Rom. i. 16).

[2] To Gentile Christians of the next generations (and certainly also to contemporaries) the argument of Rom. xi. must have been very un-

entirely new theocentric and universalistic theory, had indeed upset the expectation of the Primitive Apostles that the Jewish people would first be converted and that then the Gentile world would follow. According to this theory of his there was no distinction between Jews and Greek; but to draw the logical conclusion, which must, of course, have set him in flagrant contradiction with the historical sense of the prophecies of the Old Testament, was quite beyond him; the Jew in him was still too strong and his reverence for the content of the Old Testament still too devoted! Here at the last point the Apostle holds his hand, and instead of now resolutely striking Israel *κατὰ σάρκα* out of the scheme of salvation, he allows it still to remain, and simply turns the expectation of the Primitive Apostles right round about by a piece of artificial dialectic: first the Gentiles, *then* Israel *κατὰ σάρκα*! St Paul had already delivered fatal blows against the significance and the authority of the Old Testament. In unbounded largess he had distributed its glorious promises to the Gentiles, he had reduced Israel *κατὰ σάρκα* to beggary and extinction—we can well imagine the jubilation of the Greek, the indignation of the Pharisee, of the earnest Jew and Jewish Christian! But see! he shrinks back from the final logical conclusion that Israel *κατὰ σάρκα* has no promises at all, and never possessed any; at the very moment when the fight seems over he

pleasing. They could only pass over it in silence, and this they did. Happily the grand Pauline teaching on righteousness by faith, freedom, and universalism was so powerful and impressive as to drown for the ears of Gentile Christians this troublesome episode.

sounds a parley and goes over to the camp of the enemy! Side by side with the promises which apply to Israel κατὰ πνεῦμα, the very same promises still remain in force for Israel κατὰ σάρκα! What could this mean? Friend and foe alike must have been in perplexity! The same apostle who with new religious weapons so mightily contended against the claims of the Jewish people in so far as they based them upon *observance of the Law*, now champions the peculiar hopes of this same people under the title of *promises*!

Had St Paul always thought thus, or did he first learn to think in this way at the time when he wrote the Epistle to the Romans? This is a matter for dispute. According to 1 Thess. ii. 14–16, it seems as if at that time he did not entertain such views; and this is the opinion of B. Weiss [1] and others. But to me, at least, it is very doubtful whether the Apostle originally held such an opinion,[2] then renounced it, and then adopted it again; nor does 1 Thess. ii. 16 say anything about a definite annihilation of the Jewish nation.[3] It is possible that in religious questions the Apostle's theories might vary in accordance with the suggestions of each moment, but such variation is not probable in the case of this national question.[4] Again in 2 Cor. iii. 16 the hope of the conversion of the whole nation is expressed. But however this may be,[5] it is certain

[1] *Bibl. Theol.*[6], S. 372, n. 8.

[2] This we must at all events assume.

[3] *Vide* v. Dobschütz, S. 115 ff., on this passage.

[4] Phil. iii. 2 ff. does not contradict this view; here the Apostle concerned with Jews of the time, who were hardened.

[5] In no case is it to be deduced from the words introducing the

that St Paul, when he set out for the last time to go to Jerusalem, cherished this hope (for the Epistle to the Romans was written not long before the beginning of this journey). This fact is, as will be seen, of great importance.

If, however, it is true that the Apostle still continued to cherish great hopes for Israel κατὰ σάρκα, then new light falls upon his injunction that the circumcised should continue to observe Jewish customs. This injunction is based not only upon the general consideration that the Divine ordinance of the Creator is to be respected, but also upon the hope itself; for if the nation no longer observes its Law, then it is no longer the Jewish nation; and thus there is now no nation for which the special promise belonging to the Jewish nation can be fulfilled. Thus life in accordance with the Law must continue. Moreover, in so far as the Apostle himself belongs to this Israel κατὰ σάρκα, he also seems to imply that he, in his own person, has a share in the special promise which is given to the

passage concerning the future salvation of all Israel (xi. 25 : οὐ θέλω ὑμᾶς ἀγνοεῖν τὸ μυστήριον τοῦτο) that St Paul here proclaims a "mystery" upon which he elsewhere preserves silence. This is not the significance of μυστήριον. With St Paul a mystery is a mystery because of its content and origin, not because of the way in which it is treated (*vide* 1 Cor. xv. 51). That the argument in Rom. xi. is not constructed *ad hoc* may also be deduced from Rom. xv. 27 : for here, where the context is entirely different, the Apostle says that the πνευματικά belong to the Jews by birth ; if the Gentiles share in them, then they are bound in return to support the Jewish Christians with their offerings (ἐν τοῖς σαρκικοῖς λειτουργῆσαι τοῖς ἁγίοις ἐν Ἱερουσαλήμ) ! This means nothing else than to assign to the Jews a position of abiding privilege in the kingdom of God and to demand recognition of the same.

nation *qua* nation, and that he sets a high value upon his participation therein.

(*d*) But do we not exaggerate? Yes and no. Here, again, we meet with a perplexing point in the thought of the Apostle. On the one hand we hear from the Apostle's own letters the loud triumphant cry, "I am free from all things and all men," "I am the freedman of Jesus Christ," "I have power over all things." But, on the other hand, with what pride St Paul boasts that he is a true Jew! In 2 Cor. xi. 22 he writes: "I also am a Hebrew, I also am an Israelite, I also am Abraham's seed"; likewise in Rom. xi. 1: "For I am an Israelite of the seed of Abraham, of the tribe of Benjamin"; and again in Phil. iii. 4 f.: "Though I myself might have confidence even in the flesh; if any other man thinketh to have confidence in the flesh, I yet more; circumcised the eighth day, of the stock of Israel, of the tribe of Benjamin, a Hebrew of Hebrews; as touching the law, a Pharisee; as touching zeal, persecuting the Church; as touching the righteousness which is in the Law, found blameless." But how does the Apostle now judge of these privileges? Here appears the self-contradiction. When he thinks of Christ and of the righteousness which is by faith, he counts them as loss, indeed as "dung"; yet, on the other hand, this very passage (Phil. iii. 7 ff.) shows most distinctly that he is conscious of suffering a real loss which he only bears willingly because he receives a greater gain. He suffers loss in that he renounces these privileges because he does not observe the obligations to which these privileges are exclusively attached; that is, because he, as a missionary to the Gentiles, withdraws himself from the strict order of Jewish life and jeopardises his bond of fellowship with his nation. There is, indeed, perplexing contradiction enough here—for how can a man renounce that which in a sense is a blessing vouchsafed by God?—and the contradiction is not removed but rather rendered more complicated by the hope of the Apostle, which shines forth from Rom. xi. and other passages, that what has been promised to Israel κατὰ σάρκα cannot come to nought in the case of any Jew who belongs to Israel κατὰ πνεῦμα. Does St Paul think, or does he not think, that in the end he will also receive that promise, the preliminary condition of obtaining which he has now cast away as "loss" and "dung"? Are there thus two promises? Certainly not! But is the freedom which he has won in Christ in every sense and absolutely an object of triumphant thankful joy, or is the joy one for which the Apostle is conscious that he has made a painful sacrifice? And is this sacrifice final or only provisional? It seems to me that the Apostle is swayed by contradictory thoughts and feelings even though the feeling of excelling gain is the uppermost.

(*e*) Under the sense of this excelling gain, which presupposes the consciousness that he is raised into heights where the distinction between Jew and Gentile has no meaning, St Paul wrote the words of 1 Cor. ix. 20: "To the Jews I became as a Jew, that I might gain Jews; to them that are under the Law, as under the Law, not being myself under the Law, that I might gain them that are under the Law." These words presuppose that, as a

Christian and an apostle, he was raised out of and above Judaism, so that now, even if he still lived as a Jew, he so lived with the object of converting Jews. Of course, it may well be questioned, after what we have set forth above, whether this is a complete statement of the case. The Apostle, indeed, did not absolutely dissolve his connection with Israel κατὰ σάρκα, because he could not set aside, nor indeed did he wish absolutely to set aside a given fact. Even were he in his manner of life no longer a Jew, in so far as he did not look for righteousness from the observance of the Law, and did not usually have recourse to the ordinances of the Law; still, not only did his heart beat warmly towards the nation, but he also believed in the fulfilment of the promises to his people, and he himself was and still continued to be of the seed of Abraham. Such feelings must, according to circumstances, have found outward expression in his manner of life.

Here, then, we pass to the consideration of the actual conduct of the Apostle. There can be no doubt that he himself ate with converted heathen, and therewith entered into full fellowship with them. But this only describes his ordinary behaviour. When he found himself in a purely Jewish environment, and hoped to win converts from those with whom he associated, he, for their sakes, observed the customs of the Law just as reformed Jews do nowadays when they are in the company of orthodox Jews. For this we have his own testimony. We must, moreover, leave the probability quite open that upon purely Jewish soil he also lived as a Jew. What, indeed, was there to hinder him?

Not only had he "power over all things," but his own heart also drew him to his people and to the customs of his forefathers. The hope by which he lived was the hope of Israel—never, to our regret, did he forget this!—for that hope he lived, for that he fought! Though he had completely abolished the old conditions of the hope, still for Jews he had only abolished them as *establishing merit*. He never dreamed of dispensing with them as the given customary law for Jews. Hence in general he lived "as without the Law," but also under certain circumstances as under the Law. Unfortunately, we are unable to produce any instance from his epistles to illustrate the latter situation, and we do not know either how far he went in his observance of Jewish laws or how often he found himself so placed. There is thus a serious gap in our first-hand knowledge of this side of St Paul's conduct; but that this side existed there can be no doubt, nor is there any question of the double principle upon which it was based—the principle of accommodation and, for the circumcised, of obligation.

What injunctions, however, does he in this connection give to others? Here also we must regret that his epistles, with the exception of the important passage Gal. ii. 11 ff., leave us without information; for all those passages to which we are generally referred for an answer to this question have not in my opinion any certain connection with it. From Gal. ii. 11 ff., however, it follows that in St Paul's opinion the proper position for Jew and Gentile was that of complete fellowship with one another—in spite of the principle that each should abide in the calling wherein he was called. This indeed especially follows from the words addressed to St Peter (εἰ σὺ Ἰουδαῖος ὑπάρχων ἐθνικῶς καὶ οὐκ Ἰουδαϊκῶς ζῇς, πῶς τὰ ἔθνη ἀναγκάζεις ἰουδαΐζειν ;) ; for these words presuppose the thought that fellowship was unavoidable and necessary, and that accordingly, if the Jewish Christians did not accommodate themselves to the Gentile Christians, the Gentile Christians would be compelled to do so and thus to live as Jews. Seeing, however, that the imposition of the Law upon the Gentile Christians signified an attack upon their status as Christians—such is the Apostle's most certain conviction—*it followed that the Jewish Christians must accommodate themselves to the Gentile Christians.*

But how could they do this? For, on the other hand, they must still observe the Law, and yet every act of association with the uncircumcised rendered them impure. The Apostle does not in his epistles give a direct answer that would serve to solve this complicated problem; but there can only have been one solution: *Christians from among the Gentiles who had been sanctified by baptism and the reception of the Spirit are not unclean, they have become Abraham's seed; thus the Jewish Christian who associates with them does not contract any Levitical defilement.* This must have been the opinion of the Apostle.[1] Accordingly, the Jewish Christian is in the position to enter

[1] This can be indirectly deduced from many passages in the epistles ; it stands out quite clearly from Acts xv. 8 f.: ὁ θεὸς ἐμαρτύρησεν αὐτοῖς δοὺς τὸ πνεῦμα τὸ ἅγιον καθὼς καὶ ἡμῖν . . . τῇ πίστει καθαρίσας τὰς καρδίας αὐτῶν (*vide infra*).

into fellowship with uncircumcised Christians, and yet to observe faithfully the whole Law; for the uncircumcised Christians with whom he associates are also "Israelites."

If this were the position which the Apostle adopted and defended, then we can quite well understand that he was charged with insincerity and sophistry, and that some said that he destroyed the Law, while others said that he still favoured the Circumcision. His contention that he never tried to influence a Jew to forsake the observance of the Law—and he was most emphatic upon this point — must have appeared false! But what were the actual conditions that existed in his own communities? It is strange that this important question is seldom clearly stated in works on the Apostolic epoch.[1] The only apology that can be given is that our authorities tell us so little. From what has been said above we must assume that St Paul everywhere worked for the establishment of mutual fellowship, and that in his eyes it was intolerable that Christians, who in Christ were united *in one body*, should not live in the closest communion with one another.[2] From the very first in the Pauline communities this aspiration of the Apostle cannot on the whole have failed of fulfilment. If it were otherwise, if the communities were in themselves split up

[1] Dobschütz has thoroughly considered this question (*Probleme des Apost. Zeitalters*, 1904, S. 81 ff.)

[2] V. Schubert (*K. Gesch.*, i., S. 99 f.) is also of this opinion. Dobschütz (*loc. cit.*, S. 84, n. 1) does not correctly reproduce the meaning of Schubert.

into distinct and permanent parties, some mention of the fact must have appeared in the epistles; but their silence here is significant. Also, we ought not to forget that the Jews of the Dispersion had been accustomed for generations to associate with Gentiles, and had certainly found out hundreds of ways of breaking through the barriers of separation where these were too troublesome, and that many of them were heartily glad when their change in religion offered them the justification of a lax interpretation of the laws of purity which they had already long ago carried into practice.

But, on the other hand, it is certain that complete amalgamation was not brought about at once, and also that local differences must in this connection have played an important part. Seeing that St Paul always first preached in the Synagogue, how could he hinder —and did he even wish at once to hinder?—Jews by birth from still going to the Synagogue? The formal separation from the fellowship of the Synagogue, upon which fellowship all kinds of rights and privileges depended, can only have been brought about gradually, even though in a relatively short time, and under the pressure of external causes. Again, among St Paul's converts there was many a Jew who harboured serious scruples as to the Apostle's theory that all Christians, whether circumcised or not, were "pure." In such cases St Paul did not resort to methods of compulsion, but brought into action his principle of consideration for "the weak," and earnestly commended this principle to the Gentile Christians. "The weak" in the Pauline epistles are not indeed coextensive with strict Jewish Christians—there were "weak" ones who were Gentile Christians, *i.e.* the ascetics,—but there is no question that strict Jewish Christians are intended to be included among them. Lastly, I would refer to the hypothesis concerning the destination of the Second Epistle to the Thessalonians which I have lately published (*Sitzungsber. d. Akad. d. Wiss.*, 1910, 16 Juni). If this hypothesis is right we acquire the important piece of information that the Christian community in Thessalonica during the first months after its foundation was not yet in a strict sense one body, but that Jewish and Gentile Christians were still *relatively* distinct, and required different treatment in matters of pastoral care. Further, we notice that the Apostle is by no means anxious to establish complete union forcibly and hastily, that he accepts the conditions as they exist, and that he only brings his authority to bear in the most deeply spiritual matters of faith, hope, and sanctification, leaving all other matters untouched. Evidently he is convinced that his intervention in the details of the life of a not yet completely united community would be mischievous, and that it was best to await with patient self-restraint the growth of the community into *one body* also in its outer life.[1]

[1] The First Epistle to the Thessalonians was addressed to the community as a whole; this community as a whole was evidently completely divorced from the Synagogue; whether, however, the same was true of the Jewish-Christian minority for which the Second Epistle was intended is questionable. There is much that speaks to the contrary if one compares the two epistles, yet it is more probable that the minority was already separated from the Synagogue.

Not only the theory of the Apostle, but also his conduct and the injunctions which he gave in regard to intercourse between Jewish and Gentile Christians, must have given the gravest offence not only to strict Jews, but also to "the saints" in Jerusalem, the majority of whom were zealous for the Law. If we set ourselves in the position of these saints, we cannot really wonder at their attitude towards St Paul: he recognised the God-given privileges of the Jewish nation, and at the same time by his work as a missionary he abolished them. These Jewish Christians had in fact everything in the past and present on their side, but were of course blind in regard to the future; St Paul, on the other hand, had nothing tangible to depend upon except the force of his own progressive religious conception. *His limitation lay in this, that he had not thought this conception out to the end, and accordingly held fast to an indefinite compromise with Jewish convictions; and that, instead of carrying on the fight along the whole line, he on important points yielded to the Jew in the Jewish Christian*[1]*—not from cowardice or insincerity, but because*

[1] In allowing that Israel κατὰ σάρκα, because of the promises, held a privileged position within the Israel κατὰ πνεῦμα; that only Christians who were Jews by birth were the good olive tree, while the Gentile Christians were only grafts from the wild olive tree; that thus the whole Hope is the Hope of Israel; that the Gentile Christians have material obligations towards the Jewish Christians; and that the Jewish Christians should, and indeed must, still observe the Law of Moses, though it is now abolished! Again, it must never be forgotten that St Paul sets the νομοθεσία and the λατρεία side by side with the υἱοθεσία, as the great privileges of Judaism! The Apostle's Jewish limitations are also declared in the fact that his whole conception of universal history is Judæocentric. The grand closing scene is reached

the Jew in himself was still too strong. The logical position which he could not and would not adopt may be learned from the post-Apostolic fathers, above all from Justin. It runs as follows :—

1. Seeing that the Mosaic Law is abolished,[1] it is sinful apostasy to observe it.

2. All the promises without exception refer only to the new people of the Christians, which is in fact the most ancient; it is impertinence on the part of the Jews to claim the promises for themselves.

3. Jewish Christians who still keep the Law and would compel Gentile Christians to do the same are not Christians but Jews; likewise also Jewish Christians who still observe the Law, and on this account will not associate with Gentile Christians, are Jews and not Christians.

when Antichrist appears and—establishes himself in the temple of God in Jerusalem. This καθίσαι εἰς τὸν ναὸν τοῦ θεοῦ is the crowning act of wickedness (2 Thess. ii.). Brought face to face with the great universe, how confined, how limited is such a view! St Paul in thought and feeling is thoroughly rooted in the Jewish world; it still bounds his horizon, in spite of the many ideas he has adopted from the world outside. His heart beats in rhythm with the Jewish heart, and his head works with the categories of the Pharisee—and that not least in the Epistle to the Galatians. It is the more wonderful how boldly he worked his way out of Judaism in the deeper matters of personal religion and ethics. It would be well for the critics who (like Reitzenstein) are more than disposed to make the Apostle a Hellenist, if they would first try to gain more accurate knowledge of the Jew and Christian in St Paul before they take into account the secondary elements which he borrowed from the Greek mysteries. They would then at once realise that these elements were uninvited intruders into his scheme of thought, and that it is quite out of place to speak of their conscious acceptance by him.

[1] We pass by the controversies on the question whether, according to the will of God, the Law ever held good in its verbal sense.

4. Jewish Christians who still keep the Law, but look upon Gentile Christians as their Christian brethren, may perhaps pass as Christians (though many would even have nothing to do with them).

Here indeed there is no compromise! For the man teaching such opinions there was no longer any inward conflict with Judaism; by his denial of the historical sense of the Old Testament (*sub specie finis et æterni*), and by his appropriation of its promises, he had slain and plundered Judaism and left behind nothing but a naked corpse. St Paul also had abolished the Law *sub specie finis et æterni*; but, like Lot's wife, he still looked backwards and suffered it to remain as the customary code for Jews. And yet his treatment of the question is far more profound than that of the more logical; they, under the form of the Law spiritually understood, reintroduced the *forma legis*; it was just this *forma legis* that St Paul abolished and therewith raised religion to a higher plane! Still, he allowed the letter, which of course could no longer kill, to continue in force for Jewish Christians. The Jew in him which could not bear to let slip the prerogatives of Israel and his own pride in his nation, while renouncing the purely literal and national interpretation of the Law, and the free spirit which allowed the Law to continue as a customary code because from the higher standpoint this was a matter of perfect indifference,[1] here meet in the same conclusion. An agreement both paradoxical and fatal!

[1] St Paul already possessed, under, it is true, a rigid exterior, some perception of the relative and historical method of interpreting the Old Testament.

Fatal, however, in the end, only so far as St Paul himself was concerned! In his inward mental life he used himself up in the effort to mediate between the idea of freedom and universalism on the one hand and the ancient Jewish claim on the other; in his outward life he never succeeded either in making himself appear a consistent man, or in freeing himself from the reproach that he lived in a contradiction. But for the cause of Christianity, for the furtherance of the mission, this ambiguity in his position was probably of great advantage; for, sternly logical though this position was in its purely religious aspect, it nevertheless formed a transitional stage in the great religious transformation, for Israel is still recognised as the good olive tree into which the Gentiles are grafted![1] Thus the advance to the conception and realisation of Christianity *as a new religion* proceeded by the way of *evolution*, and the revolution was avoided which must have ensued if the strictly logical position had been at once adopted, for there would have been no point common to this position and

[1] The imagery under which St Paul pictures to himself the Church of Christ is not fully realised if we think that he only meant here to teach that Jews and Gentiles are united in one body, the body of Christ. What he means is this: that the Gentiles are engrafted into the Israel to which the promises have been made. Even in the Epistle to the Ephesians, where some passages would seem to imply that Jews and Gentiles stand absolutely upon the same level in the Church, we find in an important context the remark (ii. 12): "that ye were at that time separate from Christ, alienated from the commonwealth of Israel, and strangers from the covenants of the promise." Thus the Gentiles have now entered, not into something absolutely new, but into the commonwealth of Israel, not as strangers and sojourners, but as full citizens.

that of the Apostles of Jerusalem. We may indeed question whether, under such circumstances, even the Old Testament could have withstood the storm. Had it been lost, the new religion would have been left without root, and, so far as we can see, the Christian churches would have fallen victim to the same fate which befell the Gnostic communities in the second century.

But not only did St Paul use himself up in the problem "Universalism and Judaism": *he here proceeded even to the length of martyrdom.* On this point the Acts of the Apostles alone gives us clear and detailed information, but the fact itself can also be deduced from the Pauline epistles.[1]

St Paul, when he was writing the Epistle to the Romans, found himself in Corinth. He declares that he had no longer any place in the lands in which he had up to this time been working (Rom. xv. 23), and he repeatedly expresses his earnest wish to go to Rome. And yet, though he was at the time relatively near to Rome, he was compelled to inform his readers that he could not at present pay them a visit; for he must first *go to Jerusalem* (xv. 25 ff.). The only reason given for this journey is that he must take to Jerusalem an offering which the Gentile Christians were sending to "the saints" in that city as their *bounden duty*; when this was accomplished he would pay them a visit. But scarcely has he said this when, from a heart full of anxiety, there rushes forth the touching petition: "I beseech you, brethren, by our Lord Jesus Christ, and by the love of the Spirit, that ye strive together with me

[1] See on this point Herzog's excellent treatise mentioned above.

in your prayers to God for me; that I may be delivered from them that are disobedient in Judæa; and that my ministration which I have for Jerusalem may be acceptable to the saints; that I may come unto you in joy through the will of God, and with you find rest."

But if he must fear for his own life because of the Jews in Judæa, and if he was doubtful of his standing with "the saints" and of his welcome as a brother, why does he go to Jerusalem at all? And if he must fear that even the gift which he takes with him may not touch the hearts of the brethren of Jerusalem and improve his position with them, why does he not send the gift, if under the circumstances it were well to make a gift at all, by the hands of others? Either he must have felt *bound*, in the interests of his work as an apostle, to go to Jerusalem, or he hoped—if but faintly—that by taking the gift himself he might dispose the Christians in Jerusalem to a better opinion concerning himself and his ministry. It seems to me that we must assume that both motives—for they cannot be sharply distinguished from one another—were at work in his mind. He certainly would not have put his life in jeopardy or have lightly exposed himself in person to a direct repulse if he had not been convinced *that the recognition and sympathy of the Mother Church were necessary for the maintenance and progress of his work*; that the church of Gentiles must be kept in brotherly fellowship with the spiritual portion of Israel κατὰ σάρκα, and that for this object every nerve must be strained and every personal sacrifice must be made.

There is nothing strange in this thought, for the believing Gentiles must remain joined to the "good olive tree" into which they are grafted. St Paul, then, only carries this conviction into practice! It is on this account that the Apostle goes to Jerusalem; for this cause he not only puts his life in jeopardy, but also feels constrained, by bringing with him this great offering, to force the Christian community of Jerusalem, whose mistrust he must have known, to decide whether they would give yet further scope to their mistrust or would acknowledge him, the Apostle, and the consequences of his mission. We know the result. It justified the apprehensions of the Apostle: the later epistles show him as a prisoner. We can therefore say, quite independently of the Acts, that the great missionary work of the Apostle was interrupted because he could not free himself from his feelings of natural piety towards his own Jewish people. He was taken captive by the Jews—this is the tragic part of it—at the very moment when in all sincerity he was making the most strenuous efforts after reconciliation with them. Yet who can wonder that the Jews counted as nothing, indeed even as pure hypocrisy, the friendly sentiments, words, and acts of a man who throughout the whole empire enticed their proselytes from their synagogues and taught born Jews to associate without scruple with Gentiles and to give up strict observance of the laws of purity? His letters do not tell us how the Jewish Christians of Jerusalem treated him; we, however, remember the apprehensions expressed in the Epistle to the Romans!

B.—The Attitude of the Apostle St Paul towards Judaism and Jewish Christianity, according to the last Chapters of the Acts

St Luke's own attitude towards both Gentile and Jew makes him appear specially fitted to record the corresponding attitude of St Paul; for, like the great Apostle, his heart beats warmly *for all men*,[1] whom he considers as universally called to salvation (without first becoming Jews), and yet he at the same time regards with the greatest respect and reverence the character and the religious observances of the pious Jew.[2] Nevertheless, it is possible that he may

[1] It is unnecessary to give instances; the most important have been lately again collected by Zahn, *Einl.*,[3] S. 383 ff.

[2] *Vide* my *Acts of the Apostles*, pp. 281 ff. The most important instances in point are given by Zahn, *loc. cit.*, S. 398. The first chapters of each of St Luke's works offer remarkably telling examples. Passing over these, we find that even according to St Luke our Lord raises no objection to the Pharisees' exact observance of the Law, but countenances it (xi. 42: ταῦτα ἔδει ποιῆσαι κἀκεῖνα μὴ παρεῖναι) and declares the permanence of the Law (xvi. 17). But, above all, the "people" with St Luke is always the Jewish people, *and the Redemption applies in the first place to this people* (Christendom is the body of believing Jews, and the Gentiles are called to join them); for this very reason —just as in Rom. xi.—it is certain that the time will come when this people will repent (xiii. 35, Acts iii. 20 f.: the χρόνοι ἀποκαταστάσεως). It follows from this—just as with St Paul—that the present "times of the Gentiles" only form an episode (St Luke xxi. 24). But if this is so, there is nothing objectionable in the circumstance that Jews by birth should even as Christians continue in their Jewish observances, and specially in their practice of the whole Temple cultus; indeed, such continuance followed as a matter of course. Evidently St Luke thoroughly sympathised with this attitude of the Jewish Christians, and the keener their devotion to their ritual, the more emphatic was his approval. He is also far from blaming the

have given a distorted representation of the attitude of St Paul; for on an important point he, without knowing it, conceives of Judaism quite differently from St Paul. According to St Paul the Law has absolutely no significance as a means of salvation, not even for Jews by birth; but according to St Luke—in a passage where he evidently takes pains to reproduce St Paul's teaching in his own words (Acts xiii. 38 f.)—justification by faith is for Jewish Christians, one might say, only complementary. They need it because, and in so far as, they fail in the fulfilling of the Law; for the Law affords no complete justification: "Through Jesus is proclaimed unto you remission of sins; and by Him everyone that believeth is justified from all things from which ye could not be justified by the Law of Moses." It is not, however, probable that a difference of this kind in the conception of a refined doctrine like the Pauline doctrine of justification could have influenced St Luke in his description of the practical attitude of St Paul towards Judaism and Jewish Christianity. Lastly, the question may be allowed whether St Luke did not perhaps think

zeal of Jewish Christians for the Law. Lastly, we see quite clearly from the story of Cornelius, told twice and in detail, and moreover with special sympathy, that the only thing required from the Jewish Christian was that he should renounce his principles of Levitical purity in the case of Gentile Christians, because God had cleansed by the Holy Spirit those Gentiles who were called to salvation. No other demands were made; more particularly, no question was raised concerning the continuance of circumcision and the cultus. This is almost exactly the attitude of St Paul, who never enjoined Jewish Christians to refrain from circumcising their children and to give up the Temple worship.

of the Temple somewhat differently from, and with more of the mind of a devotee than, St Paul; but we should not forget that the Apostle, in spite of his conviction that Christians are a, or even the, Temple of God,[1] nevertheless wrote 2 Thess. ii., and thereby proclaimed that the Jewish Temple still had significance for him. On the other hand, St Luke, with all his deep reverence for the Temple and its worship, wrote the words: *ὁ οὐρανοῦ καὶ γῆς ὑπάρχων κύριος οὐκ ἐν χειροποιήτοις ναοῖς κατοικεῖ* (Acts xvii. 24). Any difference, therefore, on this point is scarcely likely to have exercised a disturbing influence upon St Luke's portraiture of St Paul.

What, however, does St Luke tell us concerning St Paul's notable resolve to go first to Jerusalem instead of to Rome? What, according to him, was the future development of events, and in what relations towards Judaism and Jewish Christianity does he picture St Paul as standing?

1. We are told in the Acts that St Paul formed the plan to go to Rome at the end of the long stay in Ephesus, just the time that we should conjecture from the Epistle to the Romans, and practically by the same roundabout route (xix. 21) as that proposed in the epistle: "(From Ephesus to Macedonia and Achaia and) from Achaia to Rome by way of Jerusalem"![2]

[1] 1 Cor. iii. 16 f., vi. 16; Ephes. ii. 21.

[2] If we closely compare Acts xix. 21 with Rom. xv. 23–25, we are astonished at the completeness of coincidence in the two passages, *i.e.* in the trustworthiness of the representation given in the Acts. This is not a "we"-section.

The Acts proceeds to tell us how the first part of the plan was carried out, and that after this St Paul did not take ship from Corinth into Syria, but chose to make the first part of his journey by land, "because the Jews made plots against him" (xx. 3). Thus the fear, which he expressed in the Epistle to the Romans (xv. 31), that the Jews in Jerusalem might seek his life, is justified by the plots on the part of the Jews of the Diaspora, to which he found himself already exposed.[1]

The Acts at first tells us nothing concerning the motive which led St Paul to Jerusalem; it is not till much later that we learn the object (xxiv. 17): "To bring alms to my nation, and offerings." We are, however, informed from the very first that St Paul started from Philippi directly after the Passover (xx. 6), that he wished if possible to be in Jerusalem for Pentecost (xx. 16); further, that a considerable number of Christians (Jewish and Gentile) from his convert churches accompanied him, and that this number grew in the course of his journey.

The last piece of information, and St Paul's own statement that he was going up to Jerusalem to carry thither the great Gentile contribution, complete one another in the most satisfactory way (especially if we bring 2 Cor. viii. 8 ff. into comparison). If the aim of the contribution was to create a bond between St Paul's mission and the church of Jerusalem, this aim would be more surely attained if representatives of Pauline

[1] The Acts tells us nothing of the nature of the plots; probably it was intended to get rid of him in some way on the voyage.

communities brought the gift in person to Jerusalem, and thus gave expression to the gratitude which, according to Rom. xv. 27, was their *bounden duty*.[1]

Now, St Luke was a member of this deputation, and yet he at first makes no mention of the contribution, and afterwards only casually refers to it. It follows that he was convinced that the personal presence of the delegates was of still greater value than the gift they carried with them. Taking into account the additional information given in the Acts, that St Paul undertook the journey ἐν πνεύματι indeed as one "bound in the Spirit" (xx. 22, xix. 21), and combining therewith his intention to be in Jerusalem at *Pentecost* (thus at a feast attended by multitudes of pilgrims) and to take part in the sacrificial ceremonies of the feast, we form the following conception of the actual facts:—St Paul, before he made up his mind to leave his mission in the east and to extend his ministry to the west, felt bound and compelled[2] "by the Spirit" to go to Jerusalem in spite of the evident danger to his life, for the following reasons: (1) that by taking part with the Jewish nation in the celebration of the feast he might testify to the Jews, and therefore also to the Jewish Christians, that he, the Apostle to the Gentiles, did not attack the religion

[1] It is true that the considerable body of Gentile Christians which accompanied the Apostle to the Holy City may well have rendered him an object of suspicion in the eyes of his compatriots, and, as a matter of fact, it did bring him into peril. St Paul must have foreseen this danger; but he was determined to risk everything.

[2] This compulsion by the Spirit expresses St Paul's inward certainty that the interests of his life's work demanded that he should undertake this fatal journey.

of his nation or the religious practices of his forefathers, and that accordingly the reports that he taught against the nation, the Law, and the Temple were false; and (2) that by bringing to Jerusalem a gift from the Gentile Christians, and by the personal presence of their representatives, he might convince the Christian community in Jerusalem of their brotherly feelings and might dispel the suspicion that the Pauline Christians were a radical sect with which it was impossible to have any dealings. He felt the carrying out of this plan to be specially urgent now that he was about to pass on to a new mission field; for he wished to protect himself and his work from the disintegrating influence of the calumnious assaults of Jews and Jewish Christians, to prevent at all costs the schism which threatened to break out between the native Christians of Judæa and the churches of his own creation, and to clear the way for the further progress of his mission.[1] The heroic

[1] Herzog (*loc. cit.*, S. 200 ff.) tries to show that St Paul's real aim in going to Jerusalem was neither to join in the Pentecostal sacrifices nor to carry with him the contribution, but *only* that he might prepare for himself a favourable reception in the synagogues of Rome: "If he wished for welcome in Rome, he must first find for himself a favourable reception in Jerusalem; if he hoped for success in attracting the Gentile adherents of the synagogues of Rome into the Christian Church, he must first find friendly recognition in Jerusalem for the first-fruits of his priestly ministry in the Gentile world." I regard this hypothesis, which rests upon a careful study of Rom. xv., as correct, though the way in which it is presented, as if it excluded other reasons for the journey, is questionable and unnecessary. St Paul went to Jerusalem also to make secure the work which he had already accomplished, and to meet the calumnious attacks which had hindered his work in Asia, Macedonia, and Achaia, and had caused him much distress.

course of bearding the lion in his den was necessary because the very highest was at stake. That God had now rejected His people (though only temporarily) was a conception crushing indeed, yet one in which the faith of the Apostle was strong enough to acquiesce; but that the Gentile Christians—these wild shoots engrafted in the good olive tree—should drift into abiding enmity with the *spiritual* portion of Israel κατὰ σάρκα was a thought which for St Paul was absolutely inconceivable and which threatened his very faith! Hence this journey, bold to the point of rashness! What it was intended to prevent came to pass in the end, and that indeed soon; yet the Church of Jesus Christ survived; but at that time the knowledge of the future course of events would have been fatal!

This, then, is what the Acts of the Apostles recounts, including what must necessarily be supplied to complete the record. Can we say that this account contains a single false or suspicious trait? I can find none, except perhaps where the Apostle is made to say (xxiv. 17) that he had gone to Jerusalem to take alms to his "nation."[1] Critics spy here insincerity and hypocrisy,

[1] No one can possibly imagine that St Paul, if he wished to be in Jerusalem at Pentecost, intended simply to spend the festival holidays there and not to partake in the celebration of the feast, in its prayers (xxiv. 11) and sacrifices. But this intention to spend Pentecost in Jerusalem cannot be an invention on the part of St Luke, seeing that he has not even thought it necessary to mention whether, after all, the Apostle really arrived in Jerusalem in time. Hence it is certain that St Paul wished to take part in one of the chief Jewish festivals; it follows that he wished to proclaim *publicly* on Jewish soil, and in the midst of his own people according to the flesh, that he still reckoned

because the offering was only made to the Christians of Jerusalem. But we may reply: that in the first place, seeing that the members of the Christian community of Jerusalem were still so closely connected with their compatriots, it is not even certain that no single non-Christian pauper received help from the offering; and that, secondly, St Paul sees in the Christian communities of Jerusalem and Judæa the true Israel, and he hopes (Rom. xi.) that the whole nation will associate itself with this true Israel[1] at the last day, which he also believes to be close at hand. What he did, he accordingly felt that he did for *all* Israel; he had ever before his eyes the nation *in its entirety*—the nation of which he writes in Rom. ix. 1: *οἱ ἀδελφοί μου οἱ συγγενεῖς μου κατὰ σάρκα, οἵτινές εἰσιν Ἰσραηλεῖται* (thus all!). The man who wrote Rom. ix.–xi. could accordingly say, "I bring alms for my own nation," without rendering himself guilty of untruthfulness or hypocrisy. The conversion of the whole nation was the ultimate aim of all his exertions. In the furtherance of this object he did not hesitate to do things which probably scandalised many of his Gentile Christians if they heard of them; as for acting and speaking as he is represented as acting and speaking

himself an Israelite and did not despise the ordinances of his nation, but accounted them in force for Jews by birth. The Apostle's own letters can be regarded as presenting evidence to the contrary, only if we assume that the attitude towards the Law which St Paul demanded of Gentile Christians did not simply express the doctrine of religious freedom, but also governed his own behaviour on Jewish soil.

[1] We must not absolutely reject the idea that St Paul hoped himself to bring about, in Jerusalem, the conversion of all Israel.

in the Acts of the Apostles, he could do it with a clear conscience.

2. The record of the journey to Jerusalem as presented in the Acts gives no cause for suspicion; but it is important to note that at every port from Ephesus to Cæsarea people knew of the deadly malice of the Jews in Jerusalem against St Paul and adjured him to give up his journey thither. In his resistance to these attempts at dissuasion we discern the same man who, according to Rom. ix. 3, wrote: "I could wish myself anathema from Christ for my nation," and who, according to the account of the Acts, goes to Jerusalem although a martyr's death for his nation is before his eyes. The noteworthy change of ships on the voyage to Ptolemais, and then the journey by land to Cæsarea, are probably explained by St Paul's wish not to fall victim to Jewish hate on the way to Jerusalem, a wish which led him to conceal his route as much as possible.

On his arrival in Jerusalem, St Paul, accompanied by the whole deputation, at once visited St James and the elders who were gathered together to receive them. The narrative of what then happened shows *that these leaders had not their community in hand* (or were they taking shelter behind the community?). They themselves *thanked God* when St Paul had related to them in detail the progress and the success of his mission to the Gentiles (xxi. 20); and, so far as they themselves were concerned, they made no demands of the Apostle. But they openly declared to him that this account which he had given them would not suffice to disperse the suspicion which the community of Jerusalem and the Jewish Christians outside the city cherished against him. These all were zealous for the Law, and were stirred with indignation by reports (emanating from Jews in the Dispersion) which had reached their ears,[1] "that thou teachest all the Jews that are among the Gentiles to forsake Moses, telling them not to circumcise their children, neither to walk after the customs."

This account, with its clear statement that not only the Jews but also the Jewish Christians were incensed with St Paul, bears the stamp of perfect trustworthiness. We may be sure that in certain instances the Apostle's mission to the Gentiles had led to the result that many converted Jews, because of their converse with converted Gentiles, forsook the Jewish customs and no longer circumcised their children. It was not true that St Paul had taught them to do this; he only demanded that Gentile Christians should be counted as "pure"; but if such was the *effect* of his ministry in not a few cases, who can find fault with Jews and strict Jewish Christians if they blamed the Apostle? St Paul, indeed, took up a position even then no longer tenable *when he regarded "Judaism" as still possible within the Christian fold, while he himself, by his mission to the Gentiles, had actually severed Judaism inside Christianity from its roots.*

St James and the elders—they had evidently arranged the matter beforehand—now counsel the Apostle to

[1] κατηχήθησαν περὶ σοῦ: they were thus, as it were, formally instructed in these reports.

take part in a Nazarite's vow, and in this way to give a public proof "that he himself walked orderly, keeping the Law" (xxi. 24). St Paul followed their counsel; but it befell otherwise than the elders expected. Jews from Asia espied him in the Temple; they seized him, crying out: "This is the man that teacheth all men everywhere against the people and the Law and this place; and, moreover, he hath brought Greeks also into the Temple and hath defiled this holy place." The last charge, according to St Luke, was based only upon conjecture, for they had recognised the Ephesian Trophimus with him in the city. The scene develops; they wished to lynch the Apostle on the spot, but were prevented by the arrival of the Roman guard.[1]

[1] There is a tragic Nemesis in the fact that St Paul's plan—which was itself quite impracticable—to preserve the Temple for Christianity —*i.e.* for the Jewish Christians—should have led to his incurring the reproach of sacrilege which was then taken up as the chief charge against him (*cf.* xxiv. 5 f.: "We have found this man a pestilent fellow, and a mover of insurrections among all the Jews throughout the world, and a ringleader of the sect of the Nazarenes; who, moreover, assayed to profane the Temple"). The parallel with our Lord is obvious: our Lord purifies the Temple, and by this purification asserts a claim to it, with results that were fatal to Himself; St Paul proclaims himself to be a Jew devoted to the Temple, and this very thing is his ruin. It was the Jews who loosed Christianity from the Temple, just as the Pope loosed Luther and his cause from Rome and the Catholic Church. St Paul, with all his inward freedom, was neither free nor strong enough to accomplish the final breach; it was necessary for the Jews to help him, just as it was necessary for the Pope to help the Reformation. St Paul suffered in Jerusalem for a cause which was not even his own —for the complete detachment of Christianity from Judaism. But in such historical situations the eye of the enemy always sees more clearly. The Jews were right—St Paul's life's mission actually profaned and destroyed the Temple, abolished Jewish customs, and did away

This account, seeing that it represents St Paul as consenting to such a proposal, has given rise to the strongest suspicion.[1] The "Protestant conscience" will know nothing of such a Paul! And, in truth, St Paul cannot have consented to the proposal with the purpose of proving that he, as a matter of principle, and upon every occasion, walked according to the Law; neither can the elders have expressed themselves quite as St Luke records; *for it was notorious that St Paul had frequently offended against the Law.* But the important question is, not the *wording of the speech* of the elders,[2] but simply what St Paul *did*! Did he take part in a Nazarite vow, to quiet the scruples of

with the Law of Moses. St Paul himself did not suspect this; but the cause for which a martyr bleeds is very often actually much greater than he himself knows, and the charge which he regards as false is often really true. The martyr dies innocently guilty.

[1] B. Weiss and others think that the taking part in a vow to which there was no legal obligation could not have proved the "legality" of St Paul; but surely one who undertakes an *opus supererogationis* thus shows his obedience to the Law in an especially striking way; *vide* Herzog, *loc. cit.*, S. 214 f. I will not deal with xxi. 25, for the difficulty here belongs to the question of the Council of Jerusalem. The whole verse is abrupt, like a shot from a pistol, and it has therefore often been remarked (see, for example, Schürer, *Theol. Lit. Ztg.*, 1882, S. 348; Wendt, on this verse) that we have here an unsuitable interpolation—not, however, in a supposed "we"-account, but in the complete Acts of the Apostles. That it is a later, even though very early, interpolation also follows from the fact "that here, in contrast with xv. 21, the prohibitions are regarded as the minimum of legal obligation that had been laid upon the Gentiles, and that, in contrast with xv. 23, their application to the whole of Christendom is presupposed" (B. Weiss).

[2] The wording of the speech may have been inaccurately formulated by St Luke, who greatly reverenced Jewish rites, either with some purpose, or through carelessness of which he is often guilty.

Jewish-Christian brethren, and could he have done such a thing? The critics answer: "Because he could not consistently have done it, therefore he did not do it."[1]

Now, in the first place, the testimony that he did do this thing is not easy to refute; for the writer who records it was a companion of St Paul and was with him in Jerusalem. The invention of an incident of so definite a character cannot well be assigned to him.[2] Moreover, the fact that the concession bore no fruit would render the supposed invention absolutely wanton in character! Lastly, from this meeting onwards St Luke is *completely* silent concerning further dealings of the Jewish Christians of Jerusalem with St Paul, and even concerning the attitude of St James and the elders. This silence is eloquent enough. The Apostle had received from them absolutely no further support; we must assume that they had left him to his fate. If St Luke's attitude towards the Jewish Christians had been one of sympathetic partiality he would have told us something more about them. No supposed bias on the part

[1] An argument of this kind is almost always subject to suspicion.

[2] Just as the circumcision of Timothy (Acts xvi. 3), which is questioned by the school of Baur (because it conflicts with Gal. ii. 3 f.), gives absolutely no occasion for doubt, seeing that the mother of Timothy was a Jewess and that St Paul would have been seriously handicapped in his ministry in the Dispersion if he had sought communion with the synagogues in the company of an uncircumcised half-Jew (so also Wendt). Besides, it is possible (certain, according to Zahn) that Gal. v. 11 refers to the circumcision of Timothy. The two traditions of the circumcision of Timothy and of the participation in a Nazarite's vow confirm one another, and show that the words "to the Jews a Jew" were not mere words and were not fulfilled by St Paul in word only.

of the writer can explain why he should have confined himself to inventing the single incident of a plan that failed while telling us nothing more; for if he wished to picture St Paul as more friendly to the Jews than he really was, it was not necessary for him to invent so detailed a story—he could have done all he wanted with one broad sweep of the brush. The narrative, however, is the more probably true, for this reason also, because it was for *four* Nazarites that the cost of the sacrifices had to be paid; and St Paul thus appeared as a generous Mæcenas whose first care was not for himself but for his Jewish brethren, and so by a twofold way might hope to attain to the desired result.

But could St Paul have thus acted? According to all that we may learn from his letters, unless we read them with distorted vision, the answer must be "yes." It is indeed certain that he was convinced that he no longer was under the Law, but it is just as certain that he, as he says himself, became a Jew to the Jews; but more than this—in *one* respect he needed not to *become* a Jew, for he had never ceased to be a Jew. He belonged to the Jewish nation; up to this time he had neither been excommunicated by his people nor had he separated himself from their communion; accordingly, he still shared in the special privileges, and took part in the religious duties of this people. To maintain these privileges and to practise these duties—so far as his special calling as Apostle to the Gentiles allowed him—was both his right and his duty. Moreover, if the interests of the mission actually demanded both assertion and practice

—and remember that he stood at this moment in Jerusalem, and that he was looking forward with enthusiastic yearning to the grand consummation when all Israel would recognise their Saviour and would be saved—he could not for a moment doubt as to his duty. The bad impression which his action might create among Gentile Christians would not trouble him; for if he as a Jewish Christian offered sacrifice and took part in a Nazarite's vow, he did not give up one tittle of the freedom which he demanded for Gentile Christians and which he preserved for himself by his very practice of alternating between the customs of a Jew and a Gentile. Naturally, his fellow-countrymen did not understand, indeed could not understand, such freedom! But the Apostle was not therefore a hypocrite; he can only be charged with hypocrisy if he had said "yes" to the question whether he always lived and would live as a Jew, or if he had in some other way denied his mission to the Gentiles.[1]

3. The following passages of the Acts, so far as the question of the relationship of the Apostle to Judaism

[1] St Luke (xxii. 21 f.) tells us that he did not do this. Schürer, Pfleiderer, Wendt, Joh. Weiss agree essentially with the interpretation of the situation as here given. Renan reproaches the Apostle with weakness. St Luke has, moreover, already (xviii. 18) told us of a vow which St Paul had undertaken on the voyage from Cenchreæ to Ephesus (this cannot refer to Aquila). The action must have been felt strange at the time, otherwise it would not have been recorded. When St Paul was engaged in his mission on Gentile soil men were not accustomed to see him adopting some special Jewish custom. We may, however, argue *a majore ad minus*; if even here he, under circumstances, lived as a Jew, how can we be surprised that he did so in Jerusalem?

is concerned,[1] present difficulty in only one point. It is regarded as hypocritical, indeed as a piece of sharp practice—and therefore as a forgery on the part of the author,—that St Paul, noticing the composition of the Council before which he was tried, should have cried out (xxiii. 6), "I am a Pharisee, a son of Pharisees: touching the hope and resurrection of the dead[2] am I called in question." It is also considered doubly suspicious that this cry should be represented as having had for the time being the effect of dividing the council and assembly, and of turning the sympathy of the Pharisees towards the Apostle. It is also said that, according to Acts xxiv. 11, St Paul is guilty of an untruth which told in his favour as the accused, in that he professed that he had undertaken his journey in order that he might worship at Jerusalem; again, that in Acts xxiv. 14 f., 21[3] all is not straightforward; and, finally, that this unstraightforwardness continues in St Paul's speech before Agrippa, Acts xxvi. 5–9.[4]

[1] Other difficulties which present themselves in Acts xxi. 33–xxvi. 32 do not concern us here; they are, besides, none of them of such a kind as to be inconsistent with the Lukan authorship, especially if St Luke, as is probable, very soon left Palestine, and only returned thither in order to accompany the Apostle to Rome.

[2] To be regarded, perhaps, as a case of hendiaduoin (xxiv. 21); but the hope can also be the Messianic hope (xxvi. 22 f.).

[3] "After the way which they call a sect, so serve I the God of our fathers, believing all things which are according to the Law and which are written in the Prophets, having hope toward God, which these also themselves look for, that there shall be a resurrection both of the just and unjust. . . . Touching the resurrection of the dead I am called in question before you this day."

[4] "After the straitest sect of our religion I lived a Pharisee. And now I stand here to be judged for the hope of the promise made of God

Even Wendt, who is usually so just and circumspect in dealing with tradition, has doubts here: "The author of the Acts certainly regards the method by which St Paul justifies himself as distinctly clever. But neither is it worthy of St Paul to confuse the situation by too general and therefore misleading statements, nor is it probable that the members of the Sanhedrim really allowed themselves to be led astray by St Paul's craftiness, and to be diverted from the plain, obvious, and declared grounds of conflict with the Christian Apostle to the Gentiles into a quarrel concerning party differences among themselves."

The latter objection may for the present be left as it stands, although, considering the opposition between Pharisees and Sadducees, and the excitable character of the Jews in religious questions, it need not be accounted as improbable that the judges themselves, together with their attendants, had on one occasion during the trial fallen into controversy. Such a thing happens even under the completely changed circumstances of to-day. Neither is it the question whether St Luke has given a *complete* report of each of the trials. For instance, προσκυνήσων giving the object of the journey (xxiv. 11) is immediately completed in xxiv. 17 by ἐλεημοσύνας ποιήσων εἰς τὸ ἔθνος μου καὶ προσφοράς, so that it is

unto our fathers; unto which promise our twelve tribes, earnestly serving God night and day, hope to attain. And concerning this hope I am accused by Jews, O king! Why is it judged incredible with you if God doth raise the dead? I verily thought with myself that I ought to do many things contrary to the name of Jesus of Nazareth," etc.

impossible to suppose that St Luke has some purpose in writing only προσκυνήσων in the first passage; while from xxiv. 24 f., xxv. 19, and xxvi. 22 f. it follows that the Messianic hope and the witness to Jesus must have played a great part in the different speeches of St Paul,[1] even if St Luke did not go into them in great detail. Finally, it is not the question whether St Luke, with special pleasure and satisfaction, emphasised in the discourses of St Paul those elements which present difficulty to many persons in these days: he indeed rejoices in them, and reproduces them with an emphasis perhaps surpassing the intention of St Paul, who himself used them more by way of introduction. No: our concern is rather with the question whether St Paul when on his trial could have advanced, and whether he did actually advance, in his defence the statements and arguments recorded by St Luke.

Here we must again remember Rom. xi. and other passages also in the epistles which bear witness to the Apostle's Jewish feeling and sympathy. The whole salvation brought by Jesus Christ was for him the fulfilment of the promises made to the *people* of Israel, *and he felt that he himself, together with the Jews who had become Christians, formed the people and the good olive tree*, while the unbelieving he regarded as apostate

[1] "Felix heard him concerning the faith in Christ Jesus. And as he reasoned of righteousness, etc., . . ." "But they had certain questions against him of their own religion, and of one Jesus, who was dead, whom Paul affirmed to be alive. . . ." "I say nothing but what the Prophets and Moses did say should come, how that the Christ must suffer, and how that he first by the resurrection of the dead should proclaim light both to the people and the Gentiles."

and, for the time being, hardened in heart. Could he now, as he stood before a Jewish court, take up another position, and, in order to avoid a charge of deception, describe the unbelieving Jews as the people of Israel, and himself and his companions in faith as innovators and therefore as a sect? He neither wished to do nor could do that! Accordingly he proclaimed himself and his Jewish fellow-Christians to be the true Jews according to the same principle that Luther and Melanchthon proclaimed themselves to be the true and ancient Catholic Church! So also the opponents of Luther and some of the radical critics of his days felt this to be hypocrisy, just like the Jews of Jerusalem and some present-day exponents of the criticism of the New Testament in the case before us!

In regard to the point that in St Paul's speeches in his defence the whole controversy is represented as turning on the Resurrection,[1] it is not at all improbable

[1] The discrepancy between the accusation of the Jews and the defence made by St Paul is obvious. The Jews brought against St Paul the accusation (xxi. 21) that he taught the Jews of the Diaspora to forsake Moses, not to circumcise their children, and to give up the Jewish customs (xxi. 28); that he taught everywhere against the nation and the Law and the Temple which he had defiled (xxiv. 5 f.); that he stirred up insurrection among all the Jews throughout the world; that he was the leader of a new sect and had attempted to profane the Temple; while St Paul in his reply simply maintains that he stands before them in defence of the Resurrection brought about by Jesus. But is St Paul the first defendant who has avoided the *thema accusationis* and has taken up another position because he hoped in this way to make a more telling defence—indeed, because it was impossible to make his defence in any other way? At all events no mention can be made here of dissimulation, for the actual terms of the accusation were notorious. If Luther at the end of his life had been obliged to defend

that the Apostle really spoke in this way. St Paul, whenever he did speak, spoke as a *missionary*; at the moment he had before him the rulers of his nation, together with a part of the Pharisees. His object was to *gain them over*. This he could do best in that he proclaimed that he was able to show in the clearest way that the highest hope of pious Israelites and of the Pharisees was no longer a mere hope but was already fulfilled, and that his opponents were in danger of losing this hope through their unbelief. Accordingly, not a shadow of fault can be found with his apology when once it is realised that the way that he chooses is the royal road laid out in accordance with the deepest significance of his teaching. It is also the way which he seems always to take in his missionary teaching. Even at Athens, Jesus and the Anastasis are felt by his hearers to be the central subjects of his discourse (xvii. 18, 32); the only difference lies in the fact that in the discourse before a Gentile audience the Resurrection wrought through Jesus forms the *conclusion*, while in a discourse before Jews the Resurrection could form the beginning, the middle, and the end. No one who remembers 1 Cor. xv. will be so petty as to call St Luke to account if he does not always mention the name of our Lord when he makes St Paul

himself before the Emperor and the court of the Empire against his Roman accusers, would he have taken the charges hurled against him as the basis of his defence? Certainly not! He also would have deduced from the alleged charges the real charge, and by its means would have turned the accusers into the accused, as he declared their want of faith in the Lord Jesus Christ and in His power to overcome sin, death, and the devil. This was just what St Paul did.

speak of the Resurrection; and he who never forgets that St Paul is *the missionary* who would gain souls will find nothing to object to in these accounts of the Acts. Whenever the Resurrection was spoken of, our Lord, as a matter of course, formed for St Paul, for St Luke, and for the listeners the efficient cause. We may even believe that St Paul, at the beginning of his discourse, said roundly, "Touching the Resurrection of the dead I stand here called in question"; for Luther also declared a hundred times that he was called in question touching the merits and the honour of Jesus Christ, while his opponents asserted that these things did not come at all into the question. Lastly, a great deal has also been made of "*I am* a Pharisee" (xxiii. 6). It is possible that St Luke has here made St Paul say too much, but it is also possible that the Apostle really *began* his speech in this way, just as he, *mutatis mutandis*, represented himself to the Athenians as a worshipper of the unknown God whom they already worshipped. In neither instance is St Paul guilty of a somewhat dubious *captatio benevolentiæ*; he only introduces his discourse with a paradoxical and impressive statement which contains a part of the truth, and which receives in the rest of the speech the limitation which is necessary to guard it from misapprehension. In so far as the Apostle believed in the Resurrection of the dead he was still a Pharisee; indeed, he and his fellow Jewish Christians were the only true Pharisees, because they acknowledged Jesus the Messiah who alone could bring about this Resurrection and who had Himself already risen from the dead.

Our conclusion, therefore, is that the author of the Acts, in his description of St Paul's relations with Judaism, is in essential agreement with St Paul's own epistles. This has not been recognised because St Paul's Jewish limitations have not been recognised, and because under the influence of the *Tendenzkritik* the records of the author of the Acts have not been received and investigated with perfect impartiality. Both from the Pauline epistles and from the Acts of the Apostles we learn that the Apostle came into direct conflict with Judaism *just because he conceded too much to Judaism.* His Jewish limitations were his ruin! In this sense he stands for a stage of transition in the history of the development of Christianity from Judaism to an independent religion. This implies no depreciation of the Apostle! Even a personality of the most original power cannot itself draw the logical consequences of its own significance; in this respect it can only work as a pioneer, because it is always encumbered with the burden of the past. We learn this truth concerning St Paul more clearly from the Acts than from his own epistles, though it is true that the attentive reader will learn it here also. It is, however, in the Acts of the Apostles alone that we see the Apostle in concrete relationship with Judaism; no such opportunity is afforded us in the epistles. If, however, the author of the Acts shows himself trustworthy in this important point, it follows that his work has in this respect also a priceless value, and that the argument advanced against the identity of St Luke with the author of the

Acts of the Apostles, because of the book's untrustworthiness on this point, falls to pieces.[1]

[1] There only remains Jülicher's argument that no companion nor friend of St Paul could have represented him as "the colourless, rhetorical type of an average Christian," such as the author of the Acts portrays him. I, for my part, acknowledge that I cannot discover the perfect and complete Paul in the Acts, but I find Jülicher's opinion concerning the Paul of St Luke as little to the point and as unsatisfactory as he finds St Luke's conception of St Paul. The Paul of the Acts is certainly not colourless and rhetorical. The portrait is indeed wanting in depth and power and in much besides. *But St Luke was interested in facts, in the acts wrought by the spirit of God through St Paul* (*vas electionis*). He did not in his book occupy himself with the character of St Paul; and he would scarcely have proved himself a good painter of character even if he had wished to attempt the task. It is not every Achilles that finds a Homer, and St Paul would have required a greater than Augustine for his biographer! St Luke gives a simple and straightforward account of the things which seemed to him important. His touch does no injury—his representation of the Apostle is disfigured by no unworthy trait—but we should, it is true, know little of St Paul the man and the hero, apart from his own letters.

CHAPTER III

THE DATE OF THE ACTS OF THE APOSTLES AND OF THE SYNOPTIC GOSPELS

IN my *Acts of the Apostles* I have devoted Excursus V. (pp. 290–297) to the question of the date of the Acts of the Apostles. I there came to the following conclusion: "These are, so far as I see, the most important arguments for the composition of the Acts *at the beginning of the seventh decade.* On the other side — unless prejudice or 'critical intuition,' things that we of course cannot search into, are brought into play—we have simply the considerations that the prophecy concerning the destruction of Jerusalem coincides in some remarkable points with what really happened, and that the accounts of the appearance of the Risen Christ and the legend of the Ascension are scarcely intelligible on the assumption that they arose before the destruction of Jerusalem. A further great difficulty lies outside the Lukan writings, but at once announces itself. Is it possible that the gospel of St Mark, the source of St Luke, could have been written about the year A.D. 60—this would be the latest date on the assumption of the earlier date for St Luke? I cannot here enter into this question. These remarks, which contain scarcely anything that is new, though much that has not been sufficiently considered, are only intended to help *a doubt*[1] to its just dues. It is not difficult to judge on which side lies the greater weight of argument; but we must remember that in such cases of doubt the more far-reaching are the effects of definite decision, the greater is the demand for caution. Therefore for the present we must be content to say: St Luke wrote at the time of Titus, or in the earlier years of Domitian; *perhaps, however, even so early as the beginning of the seventh decade of the first century*. The political rule, *Quieta non movere*, does not hold good for science. She must therefore determine also to submit this question to fresh investigation or—if convincing arguments are wanting—to leave it open."

From these words it is clear that I felt that the earlier date for the Lukan writings was by far the more probable. But it was not want of courage that caused me to express myself so cautiously; I was not yet clear as to the weight to be ascribed to the opposing arguments, and I had not yet come to an assured opinion as to the date of the gospel of St Mark.

I could not, however, be surprised that others declared themselves fully convinced by the strong arguments for the early date of the Lukan writings. Not only did Delbrück at once charge me with expressing myself with unnecessary self-restraint concerning a question which had been already absolutely determined by my-

[1] That is, the doubt as to what has been hitherto an axiom of criticism, that the date was after the destruction of Jerusalem.

self, but also Maurenbrecher recognised in my investigations the solution of the chronological problem. In his work *Von Nazareth nach Golgotha* (1909), S. 22–30, he gives an excellent and impressive *résumé* of the most important points that I had put forward in favour of an early date for the Acts, and he concludes as follows: "The hypothesis (of a later date and of the historical worthlessness of the Lukan writings) has lately fallen more and more out of favour, and is now utterly and entirely refuted and discredited as the result of a thorough investigation by Professor Harnack. Indeed, we may say that the Acts has, from every point of view, been proved to be, if not quite unconditionally trustworthy, still of very early date. And if Professor Harnack himself, with hesitation, and only at the close of his work, points out the bearing of his conclusions upon the question of the date of the Acts, we must nevertheless say that both the concluding sentence of the Acts, and the whole tenor of the book, only become intelligible when explained in the way Professor Harnack suggests, *and that therefore, on the sole ground of this piece of external testimony, the date* 62 A.D. (*i.e.* towards the end of the second year after St Paul's arrival in Rome) *must be regarded as proved and not merely as possible.*" Maurenbrecher then proceeds to show that no weighty objection can be raised against a date of about 60 A.D. for the gospel of St Mark—a date which is necessarily presupposed by the earlier dating of the Lukan writings.

Since the appearance of my *Acts of the Apostles* I have continued the study of the chronological problem, and—directed by some fresh points that I have noticed —I have now come to believe that there is a high degree of probability in favour of an early date for the Lukan writings. I am therefore compelled to attack the problem afresh and to come to a definite decision. If the solution which I propose must have the effect of revolution within the sphere of criticism, the revolution is one only of chronology—the study of the history of the formation of tradition is, indeed, somewhat modified thereby, yet not considerably affected: the decayed beams of a building are not made stronger and better by the proof that they are older than was at first thought! Moreover, in reality it ought not to be called a revolution; for the views which I am about to set forth are the result of a slow evolution of more than fifteen years (*vide* the preface to the first volume of my *Chronologie der altchristlichen Literatur*, May 1896), and the stages of this evolution have not remained unknown to those who are interested in such subjects.

1. The Conclusion of the Acts of the Apostles and its Silence concerning the Result of St Paul's Trial

The conclusion of the Acts (xxviii. 30, 31) must always form the starting-point for an attempt to ascertain the date of the work; it runs as follows: Ἐνέμεινεν [al ἔμεινεν] δὲ [ὁ Παῦλος] διετίαν ὅλην ἐν ἰδίῳ μισθώματι καὶ ἀπεδέχετο πάντας εἰσπορευομένους πρὸς αὐτόν, κηρύσσων τὴν βασιλείαν τοῦ θεοῦ καὶ διδάσκων τὰ περὶ τοῦ κυρίου Ἰησοῦ Χριστοῦ μετὰ πάσης παρρησίας ἀκωλύτως. It has, so far as I know, never been questioned that these words proceed from the author of the complete work even though they have the appearance of a postscript—the real conclusion of the book is xxviii. 25–28. Moreover, in content and form they agree so closely with the Lukan style that from this point of view strong arguments can be produced in favour of their genuineness.[1] The first impression that one receives from this notice will continue to hold the field against all other possibilities—the impression, namely, that these words were written directly after the expiration of the *διετία ὅλη*. This also is the significance of the aorist *ἐνέμεινεν* (*cf.* xviii. 11: *ἐκάθισεν δὲ ἐνιαυτὸν καὶ μῆνας ἓξ διδάσκων*); it shows that the situation is now changed.[2] Whether the change consisted in this, that the Apostle had now left Rome, or in this, that his situation of comparative liberty was now exchanged for one of greater restriction (Blass), we

[1] The construction of the two verses coincides completely with that of other statements of the author concerning the duration and the character of the Apostle's ministry in large centres, *vide* xi. 26; xviii. 11; xix. 9, 10; xxiv. 23, 27. Ἐμμένειν is only found again in Acts xiv. 22 (in Gal. iii. 10 and Heb. viii. 9 it occurs in quotations from the Old Testament).—*διετίαν*, *vide* xxiv. 27: *διετιάς πληρωθείσης*.—*ὅλην*, *vide* xi. 26: *ἐνιαυτὸν ὅλον*.—*ἐν ἰδίῳ μισθώματι*, *vide* xxi. 6, also i. 7.—*ἀπεδέχετο*, *vide* xxi. 17; xviii. 27; xv. 4.—*τοὺς εἰσπορευομενους πρὸς αὐτόν*, *vide* St Luke viii. 16; xi. 33; xix. 30; xxii. 10; Acts iii. 2; viii. 3; ix. 28.—*κηρύσσων τ. βασιλ. τ. θεοῦ κ. διδάσκων τὰ περὶ τ. κυρ. Ἰ. Χρ.*, specifically Lukan, *vide* xx. 25; xviii. 25, and elsewhere.—*μετὰ πάσης παρρησίας*, *vide* ii. 29; iv. 13; iv. 29 (*μετὰ παρρησίας πάσης λαλεῖν*); iv. 31.

[2] If the situation were still continuing at the time St Luke wrote, then the present or the imperfect would have been the proper tense to use.

cannot tell without further information. However, the settling of this point is not of great importance, for in either case only quite a short time can have elapsed since the expiration of the *διετία ὅλη*. If a longer time had elapsed the chronicler would have been obliged to relate either the place to which the Apostle had now turned his steps or the nature of the greater restrictions to which he was now subjected. It is more probable[1] that the Apostle remained in Rome; for if the two years marked the whole length of the Apostle's stay in Rome, and if he had already begun a new ministry in another place, it is not very easy to explain why St Luke did not simply say: "After two years of unhindered activity Paul left Rome and went to ——." Thus, according to the concluding verses, the Acts was written very soon after the day on which St Paul was condemned to leave his hired lodging; "*fortasse iam in prætorium traductus erat instabatque prope iudicium.*"

In this case there is no need to ask why St Luke has not narrated the course of the trial, the events which followed, and the death of the Apostle; on any other supposition, however, tremendous difficulties present themselves. We cannot make too much of them! Throughout eight whole chapters St Luke keeps his readers intensely interested in the progress of the trial of St Paul, simply that he may in the end completely disappoint them—they learn nothing of the final result of the trial! Such a procedure is scarcely less indefensible than that of one who might relate the history

[1] I have expressed a different opinion in my *Acts of the Apostles*, pp. 40 f., 294 n. 1.

of our Lord and close the narrative with His delivery to Pilate, because Jesus had now been brought up to Jerusalem and had made His appearance before the chief magistrate in the capital city! One may object that the end of the Apostle was universally known, or one may also say that when the author had brought St Paul to Rome he had attained the goal that he sets before himself in his book.[1] For many years I was content to soothe my intellectual conscience with such expedients;[2] but in truth they altogether trans-

[1] As Clemen still says (*loc. cit.*, p. 798): "His death is left aside, not because it happened only later or was to be narrated in a third volume, but simply because it was out of place here. The author of Acts had set before himself the task of describing the propagation of the Gospel from Jerusalem to Rome as he understood it; this task he has fulfilled in delineating Paul's appearance and activity there." This view is plausible; but that is all that can be said, for it leaves out of consideration the fact of decisive importance, namely, that in the last half of the book the trial of St Paul has become the subject which overshadows all others, and that it is against all the laws of psychology to suppose that the author could have been so much master of himself as to suppress the account of the result of the trial, because, according to the general plan of his work, its mention was not necessary. Clemen then adds in a note that, in spite of xxviii. 15, it follows from xxviii. 21 that the author entertained the false opinion that the Church in Rome was "firmly established only by Paul," and that this is a final and conclusive argument against the Lukan authorship. But he has overlooked the fact that xxviii. 21 is concerned simply with the leaders of Judaism, and that we cannot deduce therefrom anything that would disturb the actual situation presupposed by xxviii. 15. Moreover, this question no longer concerns us, seeing that our present investigation assumes the Lukan authorship, and has as its sole object the discovery of the date of the book.

[2] Worse than these two are four others: (1) that St Luke did not wish to relate the martyrdom of St Paul lest the impression the book gives of the friendly attitude of the Roman Government should be thereby affected, or (2) that he broke off at this point because he had not

gress against inward probability and all the psychological laws of historical composition. The more clearly we see that the trial of St Paul, and above all his appeal to Cæsar, is the chief subject of the last quarter of the Acts, the more hopeless does it appear that we can explain why the narrative breaks off as it does, otherwise than by assuming that the trial had actually not yet reached its close. It is no use to struggle against this conclusion. If St Luke, in the year 80, 90, or 100, wrote thus he was not simply a blundering but an absolutely incomprehensible historian! Moreover, we note that nowhere in the Acts is either St Peter or St Paul so treated as if his death was presupposed; we indeed rather receive the contrary impression. Neither is the slightest reference made to the martyrdom of St Paul! St Luke allows Agabus to foretell a famine, *to foretell St Paul's imprisonment in Jerusalem*; he suffers St Paul himself (on the voyage) to foretell, like a fortune-teller, the fate of the ship and all its passengers; he in many chapters of the book deals in all kinds of "spiritual" utterances and prophecies—but not one word is said concerning the final destiny of St Paul (and of St Peter)! Is this natural? There are prophecies concerning events of

sufficient paper, or (3) because he was interrupted in his composition, or (4) that he intended to write a third book (so Zahn and others). The last expedient is perhaps the most plausible; and yet even this is quite unsatisfactory, because an hypothesis, for which there is no other evidence—the πρῶτον of Acts i. 1 is no proof—and against which there is much to be said, has to be invented *ad hoc*, and because the place where the narrative now breaks off is as unsuitable as it possibly can be. The readers are kept upon the rack.

minor importance, while there is nothing about the great event of all! There is no doubt that directly after the death of the Apostles legends grew up which included prophecies of their martyrdom. Concerning St Peter we know of two (St John xxi., 2 Peter i.), and St Paul himself gave expression to forebodings of his violent death. How, then, could a chronicler of the character of St Luke have overlooked this if St Paul had already attained to the crown of martyrdom! Instead, he offers us simply such prophetic warnings as those of the brethren that St Paul must not go to Jerusalem, and the prophecy of St Paul himself that his children in Asia would see his face again no more (*vide infra*); while in all the long speeches of the last chapters he, with disconcerting reticence, leaves it absolutely indefinite whether the transference of the trial from Cæsarea to Rome will lead to condemnation, nor in the slightest incident of his narrative does he betray the final outcome! Is such behaviour on the part of our author intelligible? is it, indeed, intelligible on the part of any historian? Have those who assign the book to the end of the century clearly realised these difficulties, and do they think that they are really removed by any one of the six artificial expedients mentioned above? Besides the natural solution that the trial was already undecided when St Luke wrote, I regard, *in abstracto*, only one other as possible, namely, that the writer not only wished to pass as an eye-witness but also to give the impression that he was writing during St Paul's life and while the trial was still proceeding. But this "seventh" way of escape is blocked; for the amateurish attempts which have been again made lately to prove that the "we" of the Acts is a forgery by appealing to the analogy of certain falsified "we"-accounts cannot be taken seriously, and are not worthy of formal refutation. We are accordingly left with the result: *that the concluding verses of the Acts of the Apostles, taken in conjunction with the absence of any reference in the book to the result of the trial of St Paul and to his martyrdom, make it in the highest degree probable that the work was written at a time when St Paul's trial in Rome had not yet come to an end.*

2. Further Negative Indications in Favour of an Early Date for the Acts

Not only is the slightest reference to the outcome of the trial of St Paul absent from the book, but not even a trace is to be discovered of the rebellion of the Jews in the seventh decade of the century, of the destruction of Jerusalem and the Temple, of Nero's persecution of the Christians, and of other important events that occurred in the seventh decade of the first century.[1] We must, moreover, combine this negative testimony to an early date with the positive indication that the Jews never appear in this book as the oppressed and persecuted, but rather as the *beati possidentes* and the persecutors. How remarkable that a vivacious writer like St Luke, and one so fond of giving prophecies of events, should remain so "objective" as to betray

[1] Maurenbrecher rightly lays great stress on this point, *loc. cit.*, p. 23.

nothing of what happened in 70 A.D. and the years immediately preceding! Nay, more, at the conclusion of his book he feels called upon to proclaim in the most solemn form the prophecy of judgment upon the Jewish nation; and yet he does this simply in the words of Isaiah, which speak of the hardening of the heart of the nation; *there is not one hint of the fact that the destruction of Jerusalem has come as a punishment upon the nation!* No wonder that notable exegetes and historians have had recourse to the hypothesis of definite political motive on the part of St Luke: everything in the early history of the Christian Church must be made to look as gentle and innocent as possible, neither the Roman State nor Judaism must be shocked, and so forth, in order that the innocency and harmlessness of the Church might appear in clear light. We must, in fact, fall back upon such an unworthy hypothesis as this if it is supposed that St Luke wrote after 70 A.D. and yet did not use his later experience to illuminate the earlier history of the Church. But in reality such an hypothesis has nothing in its favour except the difficulty which has been artificially created by bringing the book down to a later date. St Luke's absolute silence concerning everything that happened between the years 64 and 70 A.D. is a strong argument for the hypothesis that his book was written before the year 64 A.D.

A further negative indication makes its appearance in the fact that no use is made of the Pauline epistles, a fact that suggests that the date of the Acts should be set as early as possible. It is true that P. W. Schmidt (*loc. cit.*, p. 35), on the authority of Holtzmann, wishes to revive the hypothesis that dependence upon these epistles can be traced in a few passages of the Acts (also Clemen, *loc. cit.*, pp. 782 f.; yet he is not quite sure), but in no instance is the evidence sufficient. In iii. 25 it is supposed that use is made of Gal. iii. 8; but of all St Paul's epistles that to the Galatians is most foreign to the thought of St Luke, and the coincidence here does not extend beyond the common quotation of Gen. xii. 3. It is the same with v. 30 (Gal. iii. 13) and x. 34 (Rom. ii. 11); the only real coincidence is in the quotations Deut. x. 17 and xxi. 23. It is more worthy of note that in Acts ix. 21, as in Gal. i. 13, 23, the verb πορθεῖν is used to describe St Paul's earlier activity as a persecutor; but apart from the fact that the word is not rare, one is justified in concluding from these passages that ὁ διώκων ποτέ and ὁ πορθήσας in the mouth of St Paul and of Greek-speaking Jewish Christians had become almost technical expressions for the Paul that once was. How often may St Luke have heard them from the lips of St Paul himself! Acts ix. 24 f. and 2 Cor. xi. 32 f., except for the words τεῖχος and χαλάζειν, simply coincide in the event they record, so that there is no need to assume literary dependence here, especially as there are by no means slight differences in detail between the two passages. The epistles contain many passages parallel in subject matter to Acts x. 43 (ἄφεσιν ἁμαρτιῶν λαβεῖν διὰ τοῦ ὀνόματος αὐτοῦ πάντα τὸν πιστεύοντα εἰς αὐτόν), but we are not thereby justified in concluding that this passage is dependent upon any particular passage of the epistles; and the less so, seeing that the expression is not strictly

Pauline in conception (διὰ τοῦ ὀνόματος αὐτοῦ). Acts xiii. 33 f. is parallel in subject matter to Rom. i. 4 and vi. 9; this likeness, however, like the whole discourse of which the passage forms part (see Weiss on the passage), must be ascribed to the writer's general recollection of actual Pauline discourses—it is not due to dependence upon *any particular passage* of the epistles. How it can be said that Acts xv. 24, 41 and xx. 31 thoroughly establish dependence upon St Paul's writings is more than I can see. As for the speech at Miletus—the very point which is characteristic of that speech is that it bears a strongly Pauline stamp, and yet nowhere suggests dependence in detail. We are thus left with the result that it cannot be proved that the author of the Acts has made any use either of any particular epistle, or of the collected epistles of St Paul—a result of no slight importance for the chronological problem. Schmidt, however, after speaking of only a few instances in the Acts of recollection of the epistles of St Paul, proceeds: "We must thus suppose a time at which a Gentile-Christian author of some importance could write about the Apostolic times so as to make it evident that the epistles of St Paul no longer work as a transforming leaven in his own soul and in his spiritual environment." I really wonder whether Schmidt will find a single scholar to follow him in this critical sally. He himself excepts the first epistle of St Clement, and maintains that the epistle of Barnabas falls into a later period when the situation had again changed and St Paul's writings had come into power again. But are not Ignatius and Polycarp very decidedly dependent upon St Paul, and "St John" no less, to say nothing of the Gnostics?

3. The Importance of the Passage Acts xx. 25 (xx. 38) in determining the Date of the Book

In this passage either St Luke puts into St Paul's mouth, or St Paul really uttered, a prophecy that his Asiatic friends would see his face no more. If the second imprisonment of the Apostle is regarded as unhistorical, then this prophecy is of no consequence in determining the date of the Acts. If, however, the second imprisonment is regarded as historical—and this is the well-established opinion of myself and of many other scholars—then this prophecy is refuted by the facts;[1] for, according to 2 Tim. iv., St Paul came once again to Asia. Under such circumstances, seeing that the further course of St Paul's life contradicted the prophecy, it cannot be imagined that St Luke would have reported the prophecy or would have placed it in the mouth of St Paul. Hence, on the assumption that the Apostle was released from his first captivity, the passage Acts xx. 25 affords strong testimony that St Luke wrote previously to that release.

4. Positive Evidence for an Early Date drawn from Terminology

To these negative indications of a very early date for the Acts we now add a series of positive in-

[1] Zahn's interpretation of Acts xx. 25 (*Einl.*, Bd. I., S. 448), and the way in which he attempts to escape from our conclusion here, are to me quite incomprehensible.

dications which hitherto have not received sufficient attention.

(a) Ἰησοῦς, ὁ Κύριος, ὁ Χριστός

The important point which we are now about to discuss has been already touched upon in my *Acts of the Apostles*, p. 295, but it deserves the most careful attention, and ought therefore to be discussed here in full detail. The names used for our Lord in the Acts are "Jesus" and "the Lord"; on the other hand, the use of the word "Christ" is quite characteristic: *to St Luke "Christ" is not a proper name like "Jesus"; he still feels to the full that it means "the Messiah," and in this his attitude of mind is even more primitive than St Paul's.*[1]

In the first place, we are surprised to find how rarely Χριστός occurs in the Acts. In all it occurs only 25 times. Bruder's Concordance, indeed, gives 34 occurrences, but 9 of these are to be rejected (*vide* the critical editions); they, however, show that the copyists *missed* the name "Christ" and were zealous in smuggling it into the book. Compare with the 25 passages where "Christ" occurs the threefold number of passages where "Jesus" is found. Coming to details, the occurrences of "Christ" are of the following character: "Jesus Christ" is found 11 times and "Christ" by itself only 14 times. Of the 11 occurrences 7 are of the nature of a formula, for they run: τὸ ὄνομα

[1] Again, the "we"-sections and the remaining parts of the book are simply identical in this respect, which is a point of great importance. "Christ" is not found in the "we"-sections; but in xvi. 15 κύριος = Ἰησοῦς, and in xxi. 13 we read: τὸ ὄνομα τοῦ κυρίου Ἰησοῦ.

Ἰησοῦ Χριστοῦ,[1] hence "Jesus Christ" was familiar to St Luke only in formal combination, for among the 4 remaining occurrences 2 (xi. 17; xxviii. 31) are also formal in character, seeing that they are combined with κύριος. Only in ix. 34 and x. 36 do we find "Jesus Christ" without "ὄνομα" and without "ὁ κύριος"; the former occurrence, however, is in my opinion to be rejected on the authority of A B³ E H L P 61. al. pler., patres Græci, so that only x. 36 is left. But in the 14 passages *where ὁ Χριστός stands alone it everywhere means the Messiah, and never has the signification of a proper name.*[2] Among these passages 5 are most instructive, where "Jesus" is found together with "Christ," but in peculiarly loose connection:

iii. 20: *ἀποστείλῃ τὸν προκεχειρισμένον ὑμῖν Χριστόν, Ἰησοῦν.*
v. 42: *εὐαγγελιζόμενοι τὸν Χριστόν, Ἰησοῦν.*
xvii. 3: *ὅτι οὗτός ἐστιν ὁ Χριστός, ὁ Ἰησοῦς, ὃν ἐγὼ καταγγέλλω ὑμῖν.*
xviii. 5: *διαμαρτυρόμενος τοῖς Ἰουδαίοις εἶναι τὸν Χριστὸν Ἰησοῦν* (*vide* ix. 22).
xviii. 28: *ἐπιδεικνὺς εἶναι τὸν Χριστὸν Ἰησοῦν.*

St Luke accordingly only uses the expression "Jesus Christ" (with the exception of one passage) *in two formal combinations*; he himself calls our Lord "Jesus" and "the Lord." If he describes him as "Christ" he counts upon his readers knowing what this official title

[1] ii. 38; iii. 6; iv. 10; viii. 12; x. 48; xv. 26; xvi. 18.

[2] ii. 31, 36; iii. 18, 20; iv. 26; v. 42; viii. 5; ix. 22; xvii. 3 (*bis*); xviii. 5, 28; xxiv. 24 (Ἰησοῦν is not genuine); xxvi. 23.

means; for he postulates it as an official title. This is an attitude which, as has been said, St Paul no longer adopts nor any Gentile Christian after him. It is primitive, it presupposes a circle of readers which was still in connection with Judaism; or, rather, it characterises an author who had not yet been forced, in the interest of the majority of his readers, to take the fateful step of treating "Christ" as a proper name.[1]

(b) Ὁ παῖς θεοῦ

In the four gospels, in the epistles of the New Testament, and in the Apocalypse, except in the quotation from Isaiah (xlii. 1) in St Matt. xii. 18, our Lord is never called ὁ παῖς θεοῦ,[2] but always "the Son"; however, in Acts iii. 13, 26; iv. 27, 30 he is called ὁ παῖς θεοῦ.[3] This is extremely primitive; for it is only found elsewhere in the primitive *prayers* of the first epistle of St Clement, of the Didache, and of the Mart. Polycarpi.[4] Where it occurs in later literature it is dependent upon this tradition. Therefore, just as St Luke

[1] *Vide* B. Weiss, *Bibl. Theologie*[6] (1895), S. 576 f. "'Ἰησοῦς Χριστός almost always occurs only where the name is mentioned in solemn form. . . . The name ὁ Χριστός also in the later parts of the Acts has only appellative significance."

[2] St Luke ii. 43 does not belong here; in St Luke i. 69 David is called ὁ παῖς θεοῦ.

[3] David is so called in Acts iv. 25. The four passages belong exclusively to the Jerusalem Cæsarean source which I have defined in my *Acts of the Apostles*; this, however, is not of much consequence here. The important point for us is that St Luke has not corrected the expression.

[4] In Barn. vi. 1, ix. 2 it occurs in quotations from the Old Testament.

is more primitive than St Paul in his use of "ὁ Χριστός," so also is it here: with him "ὁ Χριστός" has not yet become a proper name for our Lord, and the Messianic title "ὁ παῖς θεοῦ" has not yet dropped out of fashion. The Christology of St Luke (*vide sub* (*a*) and (*d*)) shows that this is not a mere relic of old days.

(*c*) Ὁ *μονογενής and ὁ ἴδιος*

It is well known that ὁ μονογενὴς υἱός gradually became a technical term for our Lord in the primitive Church (see, for example, the Apostles' Creed). The title is only beginning its history in St John who is the only writer of the New Testament to use it (*vide* St John i. 14, 18; iii. 16, 18). In place of ὁ μονογενής St Paul has in *one* passage (Rom. viii. 32) ὁ ἴδιος υἱός; and the only other passage in the New Testament where this rare designation is found is Acts xx. 28 (ὁ θεὸς περιεποιήσατο τὴν ἐκκλησίαν αὐτοῦ διὰ τοῦ αἵματος τοῦ ἰδίου, scl. υἱοῦ). This antique ὁ ἴδιος, which practically coincides with ὁ ἀγαπητός, and like ὁ παῖς is of Messianic significance, soon fell out of use.

(*d*) *Remarks upon the Christology of the Acts of the Apostles*

The prophesied coming of the Messiah is not fulfilled in the earthly life of Jesus; He has yet to come. Jesus was indeed declared Messiah by the Resurrection, but even this had not made Him the actual Messiah for this lower world (though He rules in and from Heaven). Only by a new second appearance in glory upon earth will Jesus become the actual (glorified) Messiah for His people.

Nowhere in early Christian literature do these articles of the belief of the earliest Christians receive such clear attestation as in the Acts of the Apostles. During his earthly life Jesus was not yet the Messiah, but the *ἀνὴρ ἀποδεδειγμένος ἀπὸ τοῦ θεοῦ δυνάμει καὶ τέρασι καὶ σημείοις* (ii. 22), or He "whom God has anointed with the Holy Ghost and with power (the prophet like unto Moses, iii. 22), who went about doing good and healing all that were oppressed of the devil; for God was with Him" (x. 38). By raising Him from the dead, God had given *δόξα* (iii. 13 f.) to His *παῖς Ἰησοῦς*, the Holy and Just One, the Holy *παῖς* whom He had anointed (iv. 27); He had *made* Him both Lord and Messiah (iii. 36). But still the Messianic times have not yet arrived upon earth; there is only the certainty that the times of refreshing and of fulfilment of prophecy *will come* through the sending of Jesus who is already Messiah designate (iii. 20 f.: *ὅπως ἂν ἔλθωσιν καιροὶ ἀναψύξεως ἀπὸ τοῦ κυρίου καὶ ἀποστείλῃ τὸν προκεχειρισμένον ὑμῖν Χριστὸν Ἰησοῦν, ὃν δεῖ οὐρανὸν μὲν δέξασθαι ἄχρι χρόνων ἀποκαταστάσεως πάντων*). That the Resurrection signified the appointment to the Messiahship appears also in a discourse of St Paul (xiii. 33), where the words, "Thou art my Son, this day have I begotten Thee," are interpreted of the Resurrection.[1] Not a trace of the so-called higher Christology, as St Paul proclaimed it, is to be found in the Acts of the Apostles (or in the gospel of St Luke).[2] The anointed

[1] God is only once called "the Father" of Jesus (ii. 33), and that only as father of the risen Jesus.

[2] *Cf.* Weiss, *loc. cit.*, S. 130 ff. 576.

Servant of God, who by the Resurrection has attained to the throne of the Universe, has *become* what He is through God who had raised Him up (xiii. 23); but He has not yet ascended the throne of David—this will not be until His second advent.

It is a perfect mystery to me how men like Overbeck and now again P. W. Schmidt can set the Acts of the Apostles in a line with the works of Justin Martyr! St Luke's Christology simply cries out in protest against such procedure; nor is the case different with other characteristics of this writer. Rather we must say that St Luke, in spite of his acquaintance with St Paul, remains far behind the Apostle in his doctrine concerning Christ, and in complete independence holds fast to a Christology *which is absolutely primitive.* The same, however, can also be asserted of his conception of the death of Christ. It is true that St Luke connected this death with the forgiveness of sins (iii. 18 f.), but here he had in no sense attained to the heights of Pauline doctrine. In one passage only (xx. 28, St Paul's discourse at Miletus) does the death of the Son appear as the necessary means by which God had purchased His Church; here, however, St Luke doubtless gives one of those reminiscences of the actual teaching of St Paul in which this discourse is so rich. The situation which thus presents itself to us demands that we set the date of the Acts as early as possible; for it is quite improbable that ten to twenty years after the death of St Paul a Christology such as that of St Luke could have been maintained in the Church so far as it stood under the influence of St Paul; we need only compare the

Christology of the Pastoral Epistles, of the First Epistle of Clement, of the Apocalypse, of the Fourth Gospel, and of Ignatius.

(*e*) Οἱ Χρηστιανοί, οἱ μαθηταί

St Luke in a well-known passage informs us that the name "*οἱ Χρηστιανοι*" first arose in Antioch (xi. 26).[1] By the way in which he expresses himself we are assured that the name was not chosen by the believers in Jesus themselves, but was attached to them from outside (see also xxvi. 28). *Hence St Luke himself never uses the name*; he evidently considered it as a designation which it was best not to use, here agreeing with St Paul, who was of the same opinion. But from the first epistle of St Peter we find that the name had already come into general use among believers themselves, certainly in the Asiatic provinces. We must therefore regard it as improbable that St Luke could have written during the eighth or ninth decade of the first century and yet have been so averse, as he shows himself, to the use of the term Χρηστιανοί. However, we cannot deduce from this a conclusive proof that he could not have written later than the beginning of the seventh decade. But there is more weight in his use of οἱ μαθηταί to describe Christians; *for this name has*

[1] Doubts as to the trustworthiness of this notice are now out of fashion. Χρηστιανοί (*vide* Blass) is the original spelling, and in this form it was intended as a term of contempt: the believers in Jesus are the followers of an obscure Χρηστός. A parallel instance is the oldest Jewish name for Christians, "Ναζωραῖοι," of which the Acts (xxiv. 5) again is the first to tell us; *vide* my *Missionsgeschich.*, 1[2], S. 336 ff., and Zahn in his *Komment. zu Matth.*, S. 114 ff.

already disappeared from the vocabulary of St Paul; the Apostle, on the ground of his Christology, must have regarded it as unsuitable. It is only from the Acts of the Apostles[1] that we learn that the name "disciples" —a name that since the Resurrection was no longer suitable—still continued to be used as a designation among Christians, especially those of Palestine. That St Luke himself used it as the customary name is a proof of the high antiquity of his work, and may without doubt be included among the arguments for a very early date.[2]

(*f*) Ἡ ἐκκλησία

The slight interest which St Luke displays in everything "ecclesiastical" has been rightly emphasised by Wellhausen (*Einl.*, S. 72). He is an individualist who knows and values friends, brethren, fellow-disciples, but allows matters relating to ecclesiastical organisation and to the community as a Church to fall into the background. Here, again, he is sharply distinguished from St Paul. It is true that ἐκκλησία is found 23 times in the Acts (mainly of the Palestinian communities); yet it is not the peculiar and regular name for Christians; the name ἐκκλησία is used by St Luke for a community either Jewish or Gentile (vii. 38; xix. 32, 39, 41). The passage where the Church makes its appearance in its

[1] Acts vi., ix., xi., xiii.-xvi., xviii., xxi. The "we"-sections here again agree with the remaining parts of the Acts.

[2] On the other hand, St Paul, in his constant use of οἱ ἅγιοι as a designation for Christians, appears to be more primitive than St Luke; οἱ ἅγιοι is very rare in St Luke: yet see ix. 13, 32, 41; xxvi. 10.

fullest significance (xx. 28) is an evident reminiscence of actual Pauline teaching (*vide supra*). This attitude of St Luke in regard to the term ἐκκλησία and the thing signified is the harder to comprehend the later one sets the date of the book.

(*g*) Ὁ λαὸς τοῦ θεοῦ

Here we make the astounding discovery that in regard to the use of ὁ λαός St Luke has kept entirely to the Jewish usage (the usage of the LXX.),[1] *i.e.* ὁ λαός with him means the Jewish nation; he never uses the word for the Christians. Ὁ λαός is contrasted with τὰ ἔθνη (xxvi. 17, 23; iv. 27). With St Paul it is the same, yet he does write, Rom. ix. 25: καλέσω τὸν οὐ λαόν μου λαόν μου. No such passage is to be found in St Luke. We need not draw special attention to the tremendous gulf which here separates St Luke not only from Barnabas and Justin but even from the Epistle to the Hebrews and the First Epistle of St Peter. According to St Luke there is no new "People" which takes the place of the old; the Jewish nation still remains the People, to the believing section of which the Gentiles are added. Here, again, we may say that this attitude is not intelligible in a Gentile Christian after 70 A.D.

(*h*) Ἡ παροικία, πάροικοι

From the First Epistle of St Clement, the First Epistle of St Peter (i. 17; ii. 11),[2] and the literature of the

[1] *Vide* my *Acts of the Apostles*, pp. 50 f., where more details are given; also *vide supra*, p. 67.

[2] Eph. ii. 19 does not belong here.

succeeding period, we learn that *παροικία* and *πάροικοι* were at that time technical terms for Christians and the Christian community in their relation to the world. These terms, as applied to Christians, are not yet known to the Acts and to St Paul; in the Acts they are indeed found, but simply to describe the relations of the ancient Jewish nation when in a foreign land (Acts vii. 6, 29; xiii. 17). Accordingly, from this point of view also, the Acts must be associated with the Pauline epistles and not with the post-apostolic literature.

(*i*) *Sunday and the Jewish Feasts*

We know that already at the time of St Paul Sunday was a special day for Christians. By the end of the first century it had received the name "the Lord's Day," as we see from Rev. i. 10 (*cf.* also the Didache). St Paul, however, still calls it "*μία σαββάτου*" (1 Cor. xvi. 2). This name, to which, as it were, the Jewish egg-shell still adheres, could not have lasted long; for when Gentile Christians became more numerous and more independent, it must have died out as unintelligible, or at least as unworthy. However, we still find it in Acts xx. 7: *ἐν τῇ μιᾷ τῶν σαββάτων* (*cf.* St Luke xxiv. 1). Again we find the Acts associated with St Paul in contrast to the later literature.

We must further draw attention to the fact that St Luke the Gentile Christian, writing for Gentile Christians, in fixing dates makes use of the Jewish calendar, that he refers to Jewish religious customs, *and that he presupposes that his readers are conversant with all these things*.[1] This strange fact admits of no other plain and obvious explanation than that St Luke wrote at a time when the great majority of Gentile Christians consisted of those who had previously been in more or less close touch with the Synagogue. This time must naturally have been the time of the beginning of the mission; at a later period St Luke's treatment of such matters would have been no longer explicable. Here again we are directed to a time contemporaneous with St Paul and not to the post-Pauline epoch.

5. The Objections to an Early Date for the Acts of the Apostles (Conclusion)

In my *Chronologie der altchrist. Lit.*, 1 (1897), S. 246 ff., 718, and in my *Acts of the Apostles*, pp. 290 ff., I have already reduced the arguments against an early date for the Acts—assuming St Luke's authorship—to two, namely, (1) that the *gospel of St Luke* seems to have been composed after the destruction of Jerusalem, and (2) that it is difficult to explain the legends concerning the appearances of the Risen Christ and concerning the Ascension on the assumption that they arose before the destruction of Jerusalem.[2] None of the other argu-

[1] I have collected and discussed the material upon which these statements are based in my *Acts of the Apostles*, pp. 19 ff. Numerous passages come under consideration (i. 12; ii. 1; xii. 3, 4; xx. 6, 7, 16; xxi. 23, 27; xxvii. 9). The three last passages are especially important.

[2] In spite of the support of Keim, Overbeck, Renan, Holtzmann, Hausrath, Krenkel, Clemen, Schmiedel, Wendt, and others, I have not noticed the argument that the author of the Acts had read Josephus; for this point has been settled thirty-four years ago by

ments have any weight. The date of the gospel will be investigated afresh in the next section; and the question concerning the nature and speed of legendary evolution, in so far as it admits of an answer, will be dealt with in the concluding chapter. Let us, however, at once say that a question like this, though it may well aggravate our difficulties and render us cautious in coming to a definite decision in chronological problems,

Schürer (*Theol. Lit. Ztg.*, 1876, No. 15; also *cf.* Wellhausen; Plummer, *St Luke*, pp. xix. *s.*; Jülicher, *Einl.*,[5] S. 397; Zahn, *Einl.*, ii., S. 401 f., 434 ff.; Nösgen, *Stud. u. Krit.*, 1879, S. 521 ff.). Schürer sums up as follows: Either St Luke had not read Josephus, or, if he had read him, he had forgotten what he had read. Schürer here exactly hits the mark. The hypothesis that the Acts depends upon Josephus is bound up with the assumption of the ordinary critic that the author derived none of his information from his own knowledge or from oral tradition, but had gleaned it all from literary sources, mainly those which we still possess. If this assumption falls to the ground, and if one allows him even only a small measure of historical knowledge acquired with more or less trouble, then this question whether he had read Josephus does not come up for consideration; for the number of their points of contact *in historicis* is very small, while the number of divergencies is great, and in some statements St Luke is the more trustworthy. Krenkel has simply lost himself in baseless theory in his attempt to make the author of the Acts in style and vocabulary a plagiarist of Josephus. The real relationship between the two writers can be learned even from Wendt, who counts only *one* coincidence as at all certain, and freely acknowledges that it is a questionable practice to base an hypothesis of dependence upon a single instance (Acts v. 36 f.—which has been fully elucidated by Schürer), though he does believe in the dependence of St Luke: "I see no definite reason why the author of the Acts should not have been acquainted with Josephus' *Antiquities.*" As if it were necessary to produce such a reason! As if the burden of proof did not rest upon those who assert dependence! It is now pretty generally recognised that no chronological argument can be based upon Acts viii. 25 (αὕτη ἐστὶν ἔρημος).

can never be of decisive weight either one way or the other, since we can establish no general rules governing the speed and the character of legendary accretion. *This means that the Acts of the Apostles taken by itself requires of us that we set its composition before the destruction of Jerusalem and the death of St Paul. We thus arrive at a fixed* terminus ad quem *for the dating of the synoptic gospels, at least for St Mark and St Luke; herein lies the chief significance of our calculation of the date of the Acts*—provided always that the gospels themselves do not afford evidence so strongly opposed to our calculation that in spite of all it must be acknowledged to be mistaken.

6. The Date of the Gospel of St Luke

If the *Acts of the Apostles* had been the only work of its author that we possessed—if, that is, the gospel had not also come down to us—the verdict concerning his acquaintance with the Gospel history would probably have run somewhat as follows:—This man knew practically nothing more of the Gospel history than what he learned through *Christological dogma*; at all events, he stood quite outside the stream of synoptic tradition, for the only saying of our Lord that he records is not to be found in the synoptic gospels; the few instances in which he coincides with this tradition need not by any means have been derived from this tradition; on the whole, the Acts of the Apostles is a proof that the memory of Jesus, the actual person, apart from the Christological doctrines that had gathered round Him, was at that time almost entirely extinct; indeed, the book suggests the question: Did Jesus really live at all? for, if in an historical account of the thirty years immediately succeeding His death so little is said of Him beyond what belongs to the sphere of dogma, it is no longer easy to imagine that Jesus really existed; adherents, who call themselves "disciples" of a Man whose words and teaching they scarcely ever summon to their recollection, stand under the suspicion that He whom they follow is no leader of flesh and blood, but simply a phantom creation of dogma. So people would have probably judged; for they now say much the same in the case of St Paul. Fortunately, the author of the Acts has also written a "gospel," and accordingly the whole of this train of argument is upset. Unfortunately, we possess no "gospel" from the hand of St Paul; but no one can be sure that, if he had written one, it would have been poorer in subject matter than that of St Luke!

The critics of our days (even B. Weiss) are practically unanimous in assigning this first work of St Luke, his gospel, to the time after the destruction of Jerusalem. The majority of them do not even think that they are in these days called upon to take any special trouble to prove this point. Zahn forms an exception, seeing that in his *Einleitung*, S. 439 ff., 377, he tries to demonstrate at length the necessity of such a date. There is, of course, not much force in the general consideration that, before the arrival of the judgment which our Lord prophesied should come upon Jerusalem, it would not have been easy for a Christian "to conceive of the history of Christianity as an evolution which had now reached a certain consummation," for St Luke knew nothing of a "consummation of an evolution" which had now been reached, neither does he anywhere suggest anything of the kind. For him there is no other consummation than the return of our Lord to judge the world; and the present time is "the times of the Gentiles." The fact that St Paul has been brought to Rome does not complete a chapter in actual history, but only in the carrying out of the literary plan which St Luke had sketched out for himself. In this the fate of Jerusalem comes neither directly nor indirectly into consideration.

Zahn maintains two theses: (1) He allows that the passages peculiar to St Luke xix. 11–27 [verse 27 is alone to the point]; xix. 41–44; xx. 18; and xxiii. 27–31 were conceived and composed before the destruction of Jerusalem; that they are indeed "drawn from the treasure-chamber of tradition," and are thus genuine; but he asserts that the fact that St Luke produces them necessarily shows that Jerusalem had in the meantime been destroyed.

(2) He declares that the passage xxi. 20–24, which has been substituted for the passage concerning the Abomination of Desolation in St Matthew and St Mark, must have been conceived after the destruction of Jerusalem, either by St Luke himself or more probably by the Christian community.

Zahn has not mentioned other arguments, nor do I find that any other critic has brought forward any others worthy of notice. Other arguments of all kinds are indeed advanced, but they are all based either upon the fact that the words of our Lord have suffered subsequent modification in accordance with the actual experiences of His Church (though it is impossible to discover the *date* of these alterations), or upon special interpretations of words of our Lord and incidents recorded by St Luke—interpretations which are entirely beyond our control.

As for the two arguments advanced by Zahn, he himself has deprived the first of real force; for if these sayings form good and genuine tradition, it naturally cannot ever be proved that they could not have become public until after the destruction of Jerusalem. But even if they are not altogether genuine tradition—as seems to me very probable—I do not see why they necessarily presuppose the accomplishment of the judgment upon Jerusalem. They assume absolutely nothing more than that a fearful judgment will certainly come, neither do they contain details of a kind that in any way awakens suspicion. Wellhausen (on xix. 41 f.), indeed, says that the deep sorrow of our Lord over the fall of the city presupposes that the city had already fallen; but we must remember that St Luke is inclined to be pathetic, and is fond of introducing strong expressions of feeling, so that with a writer of this kind one may not conclude that for him the scene has really changed from before to after the catastrophe.

Accordingly there remains only the argument from xxi. 20–24.[1] Zahn here argues as follows: In this

[1] "But when ye see Jerusalem compassed with armies, then know that her desolation is at hand; then let them that are in Judæa flee to

passage St Luke has deleted the polluting "Abomination of Desolation" (*vide* St Mark and St Matthew), and has replaced it by a prophecy of quite different content. This is only partly explicable from the consideration that Theophilus was not conversant with the ideas necessary for the understanding of this prophecy; for St Luke has not simply omitted it, but has replaced it by something quite different. It is indeed *possible* that the words that have been substituted were also spoken by our Lord; but if it is true that our Lord in this situation could have spoken only either as St Matthew or only as St Luke records, while St Luke gives a more circumstantial and complete form to the prophecy concerning the destruction of Jerusalem, it follows that "there cannot be much doubt that the reason of this was that the actual destruction of Jerusalem had intervened."

No one will find this line of argument convincing, seeing that here again (*vide supra*) Zahn admits that St Luke allows our Lord to say nothing that He could not have said. The most that can be alleged is that it

the mountains; and let them that are in the midst of her depart out, and let not them that are in the country enter therein. For these are days of vengeance, that all things which are written may be fulfilled. Woe unto them that are with child, and to them that give suck in those days! for there shall be great distress upon the land and wrath unto this people. And they shall fall by the edge of the sword, and shall be led captive into all the nations; and Jerusalem shall be trodden down of the Gentiles until the times of the Gentiles be fulfilled." It is often treated as a matter of chronological importance that St Luke has omitted the words ὁ ἀναγινώσκων νοείτω (St Mark xiii. 14; St Matt. xxiv. 15). But this omission was necessary, seeing that he had omitted "the Abomination of Desolation."

is possible to suspect that St Luke, because he refers to the destruction of Jerusalem more frequently and with greater emphasis than the other evangelists, may therefore have written after the catastrophe.

Wellhausen thinks that here a *vatinicium post eventum* can be conclusively proved. "In St Luke we hear nothing of the mysterious Abomination of Desolation, spoken of in Daniel, as the beginning of the great revolution in conjunction with the 'Son of Man' as its conclusion" [Yet in verse 27 the coming of the Son of Man is announced in this connection !]. "He substitutes a plain and simple prophecy of the desolation of Jerusalem" [but the desolation of Jerusalem appears also in Rev. xi., a prophecy which certainly falls before the year 70 A.D.]. "The tribulation of the Jews does not end with their deliverance by the Son of Man, but with their destruction" ["Destruction" is not the right term, neither is it the final end; the Jews are to be partly led into slavery; but when the times of the Gentiles are fulfilled, it will again be otherwise; *vide* Acts iii. 20 f.] "It is not till after their destruction that the Son of Man intervenes against the Gentiles when the time of these also is fulfilled. Accordingly, the Parousia does not coincide with the destruction of Jerusalem; this catastrophe does not form the end, nor can it do so any longer, because it already belongs to the past" [Wellhausen reckons with St Luke more strictly, and separates periods of time more distinctly than such a prophecy allows: the times of the Gentiles are already in progress; in the destruction of Jerusalem they come to their climax and approach their close; St Luke does not say how long the time of the triumph of the world-power and the slavery of the Jews lasts; but, as the parallel passages in the other gospels teach us, he could only have thought of weeks or months; then comes the Son of Man, verse 27; hence the Parousia still coincides with the catastrophe of Jerusalem; for the short intervening time serves only for the working out of this catastrophe, which would be no catastrophe at all if it had not a short time in which to manifest its terrors; there is accordingly nothing that suggests that it must already belong to the past]. "Hence the catastrophe is also described by St Luke in clearer and more direct and appropriate language than by St Mark and St Matthew. He has brought the prophecy 'up to date,' now that the original term of its fulfilment had run out and it had been shown that the destruction of the holy city had brought neither the End nor the coming of Messiah. . . . In verse 24 actual history peeps out most clearly; here things are noticed which happen as further results of the destruction of the city. From the concluding sentence, which depends upon Ezek. xxx. 3, it follows that the rest of the passage xxi. 25 ff. is concerned with the Gentiles" [It is true that St Luke does introduce a few details that are not found in St Matthew and St Mark, but they are quite general and insignificant and correspond to well-known utterances of the prophets: there was thus no need of prophetic nor of any other kind of wisdom to make our Lord foretell such things; nor can it be said that in distinction from St Matthew and St Mark the prophecy is brought "up to date"; even in verse 24 nothing appears which could not have been written in any Jewish eschatological work of the years 30–50 A.D.]. "The section xxi. 25–28 is separated by a considerable period of time from xxi. 20–24, and no longer refers to the past, but to the actual future" [There is nothing that points to such a break here, rather the discourse proceeds quite simply and smoothly: *καὶ Ἱερουσαλὴμ ἔσται πατουμένη ὑπὸ ἐθνῶν, ἄχρι οὗ πληρωθῶσιν καιροὶ ἐθνῶν, καὶ ἔσονται σημεῖα ἐν ἡλίῳ καὶ σελήνῃ κ.τ.λ.*, the times of the Gentiles are fulfilled in the coming of the Judgment and in the short period of terror wherein the Judgment is consummated upon Jerusalem].

I have given in parenthesis my refutation of Wellhausen's exegesis of xxi. 20–24. There is nothing in these verses that compels us to assume, or even suggests to us, that the destruction of Jerusalem had already happened. Everything is much better explained on the hypothesis that St Luke had omitted the "Abomination of Desolation" because he naturally thought that it would not be intelligible to his readers, and that he had replaced it by a prophecy of the destruction of the city. The fact that in the substituted passage he did not make use of more significant details than those which also appear in St Matthew and St Mark proves that he had not more accurate knowledge than they; and he had not more accurate knowledge than they, because he could not have it—the event prophesied had not yet come to pass. It is no sign of new prophetic wisdom to foretell that the city would be encompassed with soldiers, and that this would be the sign of the pre-ordained desolation, any more than to give the information that a war will bring distress upon the land, and that in a war many will fall by the sword and that the rest will be carried away into captivity![1] Moreover, verse 28 sets its seal upon the fact that Jerusalem is not yet destroyed, for we read: "When these things begin to come to pass, then look up and lift up your heads, for your redemption draweth nigh." Here everything is in the future, everything is accomplished in a brief space of time.

Hence it is proved that it is altogether wrong to say that the eschatological passages force us to the conclusion that the third gospel was written after the year 70 A.D.[2] And since there are no other reasons for a later date, it follows that the strong arguments, which favour the composition of the Acts before 70 A.D., now also apply in their full force to the gospel of St Luke, *and it seems now to be established beyond question that both books of this great historical work were written while St Paul was still alive.*[3]

[1] The form of the prophecy, "They will be led away into captivity *among all the nations*," shows quite clearly that the conception is purely ideal.

[2] With verse 28 agrees the evidence of verse 32: "Verily I say unto you, this generation will not pass away until all be fulfilled." Wellhausen declares that St Luke adopted this from St Mark, though it no longer suited the time at which he wrote! It is true that the verse is borrowed from St Mark, but it is difficult to imagine how St Luke could have borrowed it if the situation had been already entirely changed by the destruction of Jerusalem. St Luke xxi. 7–36 forms a homogeneous whole, giving a succession of events which are about to quickly follow one another. *Everything is still in the future, so also the destruction of Jerusalem.* All will come to pass before the present generation has passed away; the disciples will yet live to see the Parousia.

[3] Among the scholars who are of this opinion I specially mention von

But is there really no other reason for a later date?

There is no doubt that St Mark's gospel belongs to the sources of the gospel of St Luke. Can the former gospel be ascribed to so early a date? If two years after the arrival of St Paul in Rome the Acts was already written, then the date of the Lukan gospel must be earlier, and that of the gospel of St Mark earlier still. But do not difficulties stand in the way of such an hypothesis?[1]

Hofmann, Thiersch, Wieseler, Resch, and Blass. Plummer also (*St Luke*, p. xxxii) is disposed to accept the early date, were it not for the prologue; he cannot think that while St Paul was still living *many* persons can have already written works concerning the Gospel history. But with our complete ignorance of the circumstances it is quite inadmissible for us any longer so to tie ourselves down to one decade as to say that a decade later there were "many" that could have written, while a decade earlier there could not have been many.

[1] No difficulty is presented by the source Q (*i.e.* the source common to St Matthew and St Luke); *vide* my *Sayings of Jesus*, pp. 246 ff.; it is earlier than St Mark, and nothing prevents its being assigned to the year 50 A.D., or still earlier. Ramsay's hypothesis, according to which Q was already written before the Crucifixion because it breaks off before that event, will naturally find a poor reception, seeing that no other argument can be adduced in its favour. The high antiquity of the source Q is declared above all by a series of negative indications: the Parousia is spoken of only at the close, and in a very discreet way; the source has, if we may so say, only an "indirect" Christology apart from the pretty frequent occurrence of the title "Son of Man" as applied by our Lord to Himself. The fact that in this source our Lord tells His disciples that they will suffer persecution does not compel us to assume that late experiences of the disciples are here reflected, for the announcement is made in the barest and simplest terms; neither is there any reason why the experience spoken of in St Matt. x. 34 ff. (St Luke xii. 51, 53) should be a case of hysteron-proteron. In another instance we should be obliged to assume hysteron-proteron, if it were impossible, as Wellhausen says, to believe

7. The Date of St Mark's Gospel

The gospel itself gives absolutely no direct indication as to its date; one thing only is clear from chap. xiii.—as Wellhausen also recognises—that it was written before the destruction of Jerusalem; how many years before there is absolutely no internal evidence to show. *Internal indications, therefore, place no impediment in the way of assigning St Mark at the latest to the sixth decade of the first century, as is required by the date we have assigned to St Luke.*[1]

But what says tradition? The authorities which come into consideration are the following:—

1. *John the Presbyter* in the passage quoted by Eusebius, *Hist. Eccl.*, iii. 39, from Papias. From this passage we cannot be sure whether it was during the lifetime of St Peter or not that St Mark wrote down

that our Lord during His lifetime, on one occasion, sent out His disciples upon a mission; but we have no sure evidence upon which we can dispute this tradition, and the antiquity of the title "Apostles," as assigned to the Twelve collectively, is here of great significance (nothing is known of a missionary activity of all the twelve disciples after the Resurrection). Neither can we allow that another hysteron-proteron lies in the fact that the Lord's Prayer, even in the original form presented in Q, appears as a community prayer. Our Lord may very well have taught His disciples to pray, and there is nothing in Q's version of the prayer that is unsuitable in a prayer used by the disciples. The saying concerning "taking up the Cross" alone must probably be regarded as a hysteron-proteron. The great discourse concerning St John the Baptist (St Matt. xi. 2 ff.; St Luke vii. 18 ff.) and St Matt. xi. 25 ff. (St Luke x. 21 f.) are, in my opinion, authentic tradition.

[1] This also is Wellhausen's opinion; *vide* his *Einleitung in die drei ersten Evangelien*, S. 87.

"all that he remembered"; the place also where St Mark wrote remains obscure (καὶ τοῦθ' ὁ πρεσβύτερος ἔλεγεν· Μάρκος μὲν ἑρμηνευτὴς Πέτρου γενόμενος, ὅσα ἐμνημόνευσεν, ἀκριβῶς ἔγραψεν, οὐ μέντοι τάξει τὰ ὑπὸ τοῦ κυρίου ἢ λεχθέντα ἢ πραχθέντα). If St Peter was still alive when St Mark wrote, we must assume that St Mark did not live with him; for otherwise we cannot understand why the Apostle did not help his disciple to produce a more complete and satisfactory work.

2. *Papias* himself, if the words which follow those quoted above [1] belong to him and not to the Presbyter; these words also are silent as to the time and place of writing, but like the testimony of the Presbyter they lead to the dilemma: either St Peter was already dead or St Mark did not live in his company.[2]

3. *Justin*; he calls the Markan gospel ἀπομνημονεύματα τοῦ Πέτρου (*Dial.*, 106), but this is all we learn.

4. *The tradition which Clement of Alexandria tells us had come down to him;* it is presented to us in twofold form: (*a*) In the "Adumbr. in 1 Pet. v. 13" (Stähelin, III., p. 206) we read: "Marcus, Petri sectator, prædicante Petro evangelium palam Romæ coram quibusdam

[1] Οὔτε γὰρ ἤκουσε τοῦ κυρίου οὔτε παρηκολούθησεν αὐτῷ, ὕστερον δὲ ὡς ἔφην Πέτρῳ, ὃς πρὸς τὰς χρείας ἐποιεῖτο τὰς διδασκαλίας ἀλλ' οὐχ ὥσπερ σύνταξιν τῶν κυριακῶν ποιούμενος λογίων· ὥστε οὐδὲν ἥμαρτεν Μάρκος οὕτως ἔνια γράψας ὡς ἀπεμνημόνευσεν· ἑνὸς γὰρ ἐποιήσατο πρόνοιαν, τοῦ μηδὲν ὧν ἤκουσε παραλιπεῖν ἢ ψεύσασθαί τι ἐν αὐτοῖς.

[2] Zahn (*Einl. i. d. N.T.* ii.[4] S. 20, 219 f.) attempts to prove from Eusebius, *Hist. Eccl.*, ii. 15, that Papias is a witness that the gospel of St Mark was written in Rome. I have answered him in the *Zeitschrift f. NTliche Wissenschaft*, 1902, S. 159 ff.; see also Corssen in the same review, S. 244 ff.

Cæsareanis equitibus[1] et multa Christi testimonia proferente, petitus ab eis, ut possent quæ dicebantur memoriæ commendare, scripsit ex his, quæ a Petro dicta sunt, evangelium quod secundum Marcum vocitatur."

(*b*) From the "Hypotyposeis" (Book vii.) in Eusebius, *Hist. Eccl.*, vi. 14: τὸ κατὰ Μάρκον ταύτην ἐσχηκέναι τὴν οἰκονομίαν·[2] τοῦ Πέτρου δημοσίᾳ ἐν Ῥώμῃ κηρύξαντος τὸν λόγον καὶ πνεύματι τὸ εὐαγγέλιον ἐξειπόντος, τοὺς παρόντας, πολλοὺς ὄντας, παρακαλέσαι τὸν Μάρκον ὡς ἂν ἀκολουθήσαντα αὐτῷ πόρρωθεν [for a long time] καὶ μεμνημένον τῶν λεχθέντων, ἀναγράψαι τὰ εἰρημένα· ποιήσαντα δέ, τὸ εὐαγγέλιον μεταδοῦναι τοῖς δεομένοις αὐτοῦ·[3] ὅπερ ἐπιγνόντα τὸν Πέτρον προτρεπτικῶς μήτε

[1] This particular trait ("coram quibusdam Cæsareanis equitibus"), which is wanting in the Greek text, was perhaps inserted by the translator from the Acts of Peter.

[2] Clement himself seems to have rendered this in indirect oration.

[3] Schwartz and Stähelin take the clause from ποιήσαντα to αὐτοῦ as co-ordinate with παρακαλέσαι; Zahn, however, as co-ordinate with ἀναγράψαι (accordingly he places only a comma before ποιήσαντα). Decision here is not easy, and is not a matter of indifference. It is in Zahn's disfavour, firstly, that the words, if they form the content of παρακαλέσαι, are altogether superfluous; ποιήσαντα, indeed, is strangely verbose; secondly, and principally, that we expect simply "to them" in place of τοῖς δεομένοις αὐτοῦ. It is in Zahn's favour that the succeeding clause, ὅπερ ἐπιγνόντα κ.τ.λ., cannot refer to the completed fact; for one cannot encourage a man to do a thing which is already done, nor can one undo a fact which is completed; and, besides, there is no τὸν Μάρκον with ποιήσαντα, as we should expect were Schwartz correct. And yet it is not difficult to suppose that the last clause passes over the preceding clause and connects with the next but one, so that the clause between is to be regarded as a kind of parenthesis. Schwartz's punctuation is therefore probably correct. The subsequent occurrence of προτρεπτικῶς with προτρέψασθαι is unusual, but not impossible. Schwartz would read πνευματικῶς, which would go with ἐπιγνόντα, and receives strong support from ii. 15 (Schwartz, Bd. I. S. 140, 11).

κωλῦσαι μήτε προτρέψασθαι. I need not enter into an investigation concerning the relation between these two accounts, which are really one and the same. Here for the first time we learn that the gospel of St Mark was written by St Mark in Rome when St Peter was yet alive, at the request of the hearers of St Peter; that St Peter, however, was quite indifferent in the matter. This last remark can only have been occasioned by an opinion concerning the book, similar to that reported by Papias and John the Presbyter; *i.e.* because of certain faults in the gospel it was considered incredible that the book could have received the approbation of St Peter (which would have made it his own), though it was not desired that the use of the gospel should be otherwise discouraged. The tradition springs from a time when the book had not yet attained to canonical dignity. Even then it was thought that the book was written at Rome during the lifetime of St Peter.[1]

5. *Irenæus*; he writes (iii. 1, 1; the Greek is found in Euseb., *Hist. Eccl.*, v. 8, 2): Ὁ μὲν δὴ Ματθαῖος ἐν τοῖς Ἑβραίοις τῇ ἰδίᾳ αὐτῶν διαλέκτῳ καὶ γραφὴν ἐξήνεγκεν εὐαγγελίου, τοῦ Πέτρου καὶ τοῦ Παύλου ἐν Ῥώμῃ εὐαγγελιζομένων καὶ θεμελιούντων τὴν ἐκκλησίαν, μετὰ δὲ τὴν τούτων ἔξοδον Μάρκος, ὁ μαθητὴς καὶ ἑρμηνευτὴς Πέτρου, καὶ αὐτὸς τὰ ὑπὸ Πέτρου κηρυσ-

[1] Eusebius also notices this tradition, which he derived from St Clement, in his second book (chap. xv.), before he gives it in his sixth book; in the former passage he interpolates a later tradition, which is introduced by φασι, and is irreconcilable with St Clement. It runs: γνόντα δὲ τὸ πραχθέν φασι τὸν ἀπόστολον ἀποκαλύψαντος αὐτῷ τοῦ πνεύματος ἡσθῆναι τῇ τῶν ἀνδρῶν προθυμίᾳ κυρῶσαί τε τὴν γραφὴν εἰς ἔντευξιν ταῖς ἐκκλησίαις.

σόμενα ἐγγράφως ἡμῖν παραδέδωκεν. καὶ Λουκᾶς δέ, ὁ ἀκόλουθος Παύλου, τὸ ὑπ' ἐκείνου κηρυσσόμενον εὐαγγέλιον ἐν βίβλῳ κατέθετο. ἔπειτα Ἰωάννης ὁ μαθητὴς τοῦ κυρίου, ὁ καὶ ἐπὶ τὸ στῆθος αὐτοῦ ἀναπεσών, καὶ αὐτὸς ἐξέδωκε τὸ εὐαγγέλιον, ἐν Ἐφέσῳ τῆς Ἀσίας διατρίβων.

To Chapman (*Journal of Theol. Stud.*, 1905, July, pp. 563 ff.) belongs the credit of having first correctly interpreted this passage, which hitherto had been a veritable *crux*, because it did not seem to fit in with the other chronological traditions. Chapman has shown that it is not the intention of the writer to give us in this passage any chronological information concerning the origin of the gospels apart from the incidental remark that the fourth gospel is the latest; such information, indeed, is not given in the case of the third and fourth gospels. The context of the passage, which should be carefully studied, shows that Irenæus simply wished to prove that the teaching of the four chief apostles did not perish with their death, but that it has come down to us in writing. How did this happen? The answer given by Irenæus is stated in the passage quoted above. Taking the context into consideration this passage may be paraphrased as follows: "*Among the Hebrews, Matthew* also published in their own tongue a *written* gospel [besides his oral teaching], while[1] *in Rome Peter and Paul* proclaimed [orally, not in writing] the Gospel, and founded the Church. But [although they died without leaving behind them a written gospel, their

[1] The genitive Absolute is not temporal; it does not imply that the gospel of St Matthew was written at that time; it simply contrasts the ministry of the two great Apostles with that of St Matthew.

teaching has not perished, for] after their death *Mark* also [like Matthew], the disciple and interpreter of Peter, handed down to us in writing the teaching of *Peter*; and *Luke*, the follower of *Paul*, gathered together in a *book* the Gospel preached by the latter apostle. Thereupon *John*, the disciple of the Lord, who also lay in his bosom, he also published the Gospel while he was dwelling at *Ephesus*."

Irenæus does not mean to say that the gospel of St Matthew was composed at the time when St Peter and St Paul were preaching in Rome, nor that the second gospel was not written until after the death of the two chief apostles. He had no further information concerning the origin of the two gospels than what could be read in Papias, upon whose words his own are based. All that is additional is only in seeming, but Irenæus did not even intend to give an appearance of more detailed knowledge.

6. There are numerous other later authorities who give Rome as the birthplace of the gospel,[1] and still more numerous are those who mention the names of St Peter and St Mark in closest combination in connection with its composition; but it is improbable that any one of these later authorities represents a tradition that is independent of the earlier authorities.

Of the traditions which we have here collected together the following seem to me to be worthy of notice: (1) that St Mark in his gospel made use of

[1] Chrysostom makes an exception; but his statement that St Mark wrote his gospel at the request of his hearers in Egypt is probably only due to a confusion of two traditions—a confusion that could easily have been made.

tradition, some of which, at all events, was derived from St Peter[1]; (2) that St Peter had nothing whatever to do with the composition of the gospel; and (3) that the gospel was edited and published in Rome. We view with great suspicion the tradition recorded by St Clement that St Mark had begun his gospel while St Peter was alive, but at first without his knowledge; and that St Peter, when the fact came to his notice, did not interfere either by way of encouragement or discouragement. This legend looks just like one that has been invented to explain striking characteristics of the gospel, such as its omissions (*vide* John the Presbyter, Papias). If we are right in this opinion, then the report that St Mark wrote his gospel in Rome by request, especially as the Presbyter and Papias say nothing of it, cannot pass unchallenged; for it is bound up with a legend that has a distinct purpose. and it would almost necessarily grow out of the fact that the gospel was *officially edited and published* in Rome. It is possible that St Mark brought his gospel to Rome when he came thither to St Paul in prison; he may, while in Rome, have subjected it to further revision, and some considerable time later may have published it at the prayer of the Roman Christians. Only then would this prayer have been in place. Of course, it may have been that St Mark started writing the gospel in Rome, but this is not necessarily required by the tradition.[2]

[1] It is true that the internal character of the gospel justifies this tradition, if at all, only to a very restricted extent.

[2] Wellhausen (*loc. cit.*, S. 87) writes: "So far as we depend upon

If we compare this conclusion from the evidence of tradition with the date presupposed by the chronology of the Lukan writings, we find that they are not contradictory. Tradition asserts no veto against the hypothesis that St Luke, when he met St Mark in the company of St Paul the prisoner, was permitted by him to peruse a written record of the Gospel history which was essentially identical with the gospel of St Mark given to the Church at a later time; indeed, the peculiar relation that exists between our second and third gospels suggests that St Luke was not yet acquainted with St Mark's final revision, which, as we can quite well imagine, St Mark undertook while in Rome. Seeing, then, that tradition, though it does not actually support, nevertheless does not contradict the view, gained from our investigation of the Lukan writings, that St Mark must have written his gospel during the sixth decade of the first century at the latest, this date may be regarded as certain.[1]

8. The Date of St Matthew's Gospel

In regard to the date of the first gospel I have nothing new to add to what I have already written in

conjecture, Jerusalem alone comes into consideration as the place of writing. We have reason to conjecture that the tradition was first written down in the place where it had its centre as oral tradition." (Wellhausen also refers to xv. 21, which others have brought forward as evidence for the composition in Rome.) Wellhausen, it seems to me, goes too far here.

[1] The decided Paulinism of the author contributes to fix a *terminus a quo* for the date of the gospel.

my *Chronologie*, i., S. 653 f.[1] The book must be placed in close proximity with the destruction of Jerusalem. In its present shape, however, it should be assigned to the years immediately succeeding that catastrophe. Here St Matt. xxii. 7 (a verse wanting in St Luke) is of special weight. And yet composition before the catastrophe cannot be excluded with absolute certainty.[2] Moreover, the first gospel more than any other of the synoptics, and in course of a more considerable period of time, has suffered from serious and repeated interpolation.[3] That the synoptic gospel which was most

[1] On the other hand, my views in that work, as to the date of St Mark, receive severe correction.

[2] In *Chronol.*, i., S. 654, n. 1, I have written: "I could sooner convince myself that Matthew was written before the destruction of Jerusalem than believe that one decade elapsed after the catastrophe before the book was written." Chap. xxvii. 8 and many other passages are rather in favour of composition before the catastrophe.

[3] As evidence that St Matthew was little known in Rome, even at the beginning of the second century, we have a piece of external testimony, though indeed it is not quite clear; I mean that remarkable note of Eusebius (Pseudo-Eusebius), preserved in the Syriac, concerning the star of the Magi (Nestle, *Marginalien und Materialien*, S. 72; *cf.* my *Chronologie*, ii., S. 126): "In the second year of our Lord, during the consulship of Cæsar and Capito, in the month Kanun II, these Magi came from the East and paid homage to our Lord. And in the year 430 (beginning Oct. 1, 118), during the reign of Hadrian, during the consulship of Severus and Fulgus [Fulvus] (ann. 120), and the episcopate of Xystus, bishop of the city of Rome (about 120), question as to this arose among the people who were acquainted with the Holy Scriptures, and through the efforts of great men in different places the history of this fact was sought for and found, and was written in the language of those who cared for it." From this obscure record we may, it appears, conclude so much at least, that in the year 120 A.D. St Matthew was not a book that was universally known and read in the Church of Rome.

read should have received the most numerous accretions, and should be the latest in date, is nothing remarkable, but only natural. Moreover, it remains, in regard to *form*, the oldest "book of the Gospel"; the others have obtained the rank and dignity of such a title because they have been set by the side of St Matthew's gospel, which from the first, unlike the others, claims to be an ecclesiastical book. As the place of origin of the first gospel, Palestine alone can come into consideration; in that country it was the book of the liberal Jewish Christians, who stood in sharp opposition to the Scribes and Pharisees. Thus the book cannot have arisen among those "myriads" of Jewish Christians who encountered St Paul on his last visit, and were all zealous for the Law, but among the circles of Hellenistic Jewish Christians who dwelt in Jerusalem and Palestine, who traced their spiritual descent to St Stephen, and from whose midst proceeded those missionaries who first (in Antioch) preached the Gospel to the Gentiles. By such Christians, who left Palestine after the great catastrophe, the gospel of St Matthew was brought to Asia Minor and other Christian centres.[1]

[1] In the preceding section we have shown that Irenæus gives no information concerning the date of the first gospel (except for the fact that he places St Matthew at the head of the four gospels).

CHAPTER IV

THE PRIMITIVE LEGENDS OF CHRISTENDOM

"THE tradition which St Mark chronicles is comparatively rich in its reference to Jerusalem, while it is comparatively poor in its reference to Galilee. This fact cannot be easily explained if the tradition was originally derived from the first disciples. Neither are the Galilean stories of such a character that they can be referred to these authorities. . . . Rather it seems that the narrative in St Mark did not for the most part proceed from the intimate friends of Jesus. This narrative has, for the most part, a somewhat rude popular character, such as it would have gathered during a considerable period of circulation by word of mouth among the common people before it attained to the unaffectedly drastic form in which it now lies before us" (Wellhausen, *Einleit.*, S. 52 f.). These are the words of a champion who has delivered us from the tyranny of those feeble and artificial theories which attempt to base either St Mark as a whole or a great part of the gospel upon the testimony of St Peter. Wellhausen has, moreover, shown in his commentary how seldom in the stories of St Mark there is ground for concluding that they are based upon direct tradition. The traditions they record are second-hand and third-hand, though indeed their growth must have been rapid; and these traditions, so multifarious and different in character, clearly show that they are combined from different sources. And yet the sources all lie in the homeland of Palestine, nothing comes from outside, from the Christian Diaspora; still less can one point to the sphere of "Gentile" influence. It is highly remarkable that the Old Testament plays scarcely any part in this tradition, *i.e.* it is not determined or dominated by the motive to discover in our Lord's life as many instances as possible of prophecy fulfilled! We, indeed, are struck by the absence of reference to the Old Testament; certain traits in the history of the Passion, even in St Mark, possibly form an exception, but with our present knowledge we are no longer able to decide whether, and to what extent, certain passages of the Prophets and Psalms have exercised influence upon this part of the Gospel history. Not everything that seems to be due need be due to such an influence. Supposing that no tradition had come down to us concerning the author of the second gospel, we should have conjectured that he was a native of Jerusalem, who had not himself seen Jesus, and indeed was also probably too young to have received and preserved any impression of Him, who nevertheless may have come into touch with our Lord's personal disciples, though he wrote his gospel neither by their direction nor mainly upon the authority of their records. Seeing that he wished to tell of Jesus, and to picture Him as the

Son of God, he had no need to confine himself with scrupulous care to the "best" sources. From the manifold traditions that were current he chose and threw into form those that best suited his purpose. It is otherwise with the source Q. Here one receives the impression that a personal disciple of our Lord has written down all the teaching of Jesus which seemed to him most important for the life of discipleship. He felt that a collection should be made of the "Maxims" of the Teacher, who was more than a teacher or a prophet, and yet remained the Teacher though he was and is something much higher. It is not necessary to assume that one of the Twelve made the collection, but there is also nothing to exclude such an hypothesis. Q seems to have included only two real legends—the Divine Voice at the Baptism and the story of the Temptation —but we do not know whether these belonged to the original form of Q. They at all events were in Q as it lay before the authors of the first and third gospels. The version of the Voice at the Baptism in Q shows that its author based our Lord's Messiahship upon this event ("Thou art my Son, this day have I begotten Thee"). The story of the Temptation is, as is shown by the change of scene, an artificial composition; its purpose in Q is to show our Lord approving Himself as the Son of God at the beginning of His ministry; but the situation implied in the second and third assaults of the Tempter belongs, as it seems, to the last weeks of our Lord's life (perhaps in Jerusalem). There it would be in its historical setting. A parallel instance to the hysteron-proteron here occurring in Q, is to be found in the fourth gospel, where the

Cleansing of the Temple is transferred to the beginning of the ministry of our Lord. Besides this passage and the questionable use of the title "Son of Man," the source affords only very little, indeed nothing of importance, that does not belong to first-hand tradition and does not bear the stamp of trustworthiness (against Wellhausen, whose objections proceed from his tendency to limit too strictly what was possible for the historical Jesus [1]). Q, therefore, does not come within the scope of our inquiry concerning the formation of legend.

The question whether the occurrence of legends and later traditions in the first three gospels harmonises with the date we have assigned to them can therefore only refer to the material that is peculiar to St Matthew and to St Luke, as well as to the transformations which Q and St Mark experience in these gospels. As for the changes in Q and St Mark, there is nothing to be found in them that can disturb our belief in the correctness of our chronology. Neither the careful examination which Wellhausen has made in his *Einleitung* into the question of the treatment of Q in St Luke and St Matthew, nor my own investigations in *The Sayings of Jesus*, have led to any results which compel us to assign a later date to these gospels.[2] It is quite obvious

[1] Wellhausen disputes, for example (*loc. cit.*, S. 87), that our Lord during His lifetime sent out His disciples as Apostles; but St Paul has handed down to us a saying, as a *word of our Lord* (1 Cor. ix. 14), that it is right that οἱ τὸ εὐαγγέλιον καταγγέλλοντες ἐκ τοῦ εὐαγγελίου ζῆν. This saying at the same time testifies to our Lord's use of the term "Gospel."

[2] Wellhausen's criticism does not always distinguish quite accurately between what belongs to Q and what belongs to the evangelist, and

that in St Matthew numerous hystera-protera are to be found; none, however, that are of a blatant character. It is, indeed, a fact that in this gospel our Lord is represented as giving charges and directions to a definitely formed community, but there is absolutely nothing to show that this anachronism could not have been committed so early as twenty years after Pentecost; only think how St Paul speaks of Christ and the Church! In St Luke, however, in spite of the numerous alterations and corrections of the text of St Mark and of Q, absolutely nothing is to be found that compels us to assume a later date; all these alterations are for the most part stylistic, and where they pass beyond style we encounter nothing upon which we can base an argument for bringing down the composition of the gospel to a later period.

Hence there remains only the subject-matter peculiar to St Matthew and to St Luke. Where this consists of new *sayings, discourses, parables, and stories*, the same remarks apply as in the case of the corrections of Q and St Mark, although this new material bears for the most part the stamp of second-hand or third-hand tradition. No one can maintain that these traditions cannot have taken their present form until after the destruction of Jerusalem, or at least until after the year 60 A.D.[1]

this circumstance has contributed to make his verdict on Q more unfavourable; it, however, does not affect the question how late the gospels fall.

[1] Misguided attempts have indeed been made to prove that in some of these passages there are historical references to events that occurred in the last quarter of the first century, or at the beginning of the second. These attempts are scarcely mentioned nowadays.

Neither can it be proved that they bear the trace of foreign, extra-Palestinian, influence. We may therefore leave them out of consideration. Accordingly, we are concerned with only the following passages :—

1. The story of the Infancy in St Matthew, chaps. i., ii.[1]
2. The commission to St Peter, chap. xvi. 17–19.
3. The words concerning the practice of discipline in the community, xviii. 15–17.
4. The death of Judas, etc., xxvii. 3–10.
5. The wife of Pilate, xxvii. 19.
6. Pilate and the people, xxvii. 24 f.
7. The miracles at our Lord's death, xxvii. 51–53.
8. The watch at the grave, xxvii. 62–66; xxviii. 11–15.
9. The angel who rolls away the stone, xxviii. 2 f.
10. The appearance of our Lord to the women, xxviii. 9 f.
11. The appearance of our Lord to the eleven disciples, xxviii. 16 f.

(*a*) The story of the Infancy in St Luke i., ii., iii. 23–38.[2]

(*b*) St Peter's draught of fishes, St Luke v. 4–9.

(*c*) The woman who was a sinner, vii. 36–50.

(*d*) A woman's exclamation concerning the blessedness of the mother of our Lord, xi. 27 f.

(*e*) Our Lord before Herod, xxiii. 6–12.

[1] I do not intend here to prove afresh that these chapters have from the beginning formed part of the first gospel.

[2] It is certain that these passages ought not (as with Marcion) to be eliminated from the third gospel.

(*f*) Our Lord and the women on the way to Golgotha, xxiii. 27–31.
(*g*) The thief upon the cross, xxiii. 39–43; also the words from the cross, xxiii. 34 and 46.
(*h*) The journey to Emmaus, xxiv. 13–35.
(*i*) The conclusion of the stories of the Resurrection, xxiv. 36–53.
(*k*) The converse of our Lord with His disciples after His Resurrection; and His Ascension, Acts i.

Let us take first the passages peculiar to St Matthew. Here the story of the Infancy, chaps. i. and ii., is often said to be of very late date; indeed, by many critics it is brought down into the second century and its Palestinian origin is denied. But, the episode of the Magi (ii. 1–12) being left for the present out of consideration, there are three circumstances that commend caution: in the first place, the conception of Pre-existence is entirely absent; secondly, the newly-born "Jesus" is so named because He will save "His nation" (this nation alone is spoken of in i. 21); thirdly, the whole narrative breathes of Palestine, and is constructed so as to fit exactly into the scheme of fulfilment of Old Testament prophecy. Critics may call this narrative late, but in saying this they only express the fact that they find themselves out of sympathy with it; and to be in sympathy with a narrative of this kind is especially difficult for us Westerns of the nineteenth and twentieth centuries!

A story of the birth of our Lord, that had grown up freely in Gentile-Christian soil about the years 50 or 80 or 100 A.D., would certainly have been of quite a different character from the story of the first gospel! To say nothing of the genealogy (i. 1–17)—which, both in its whole structure as well as by the amazing boldness of its mention of Tamar and the wife of Uriah, becomes the less intelligible the later the date one assigns to it—who can fail to recognise that the first evangelist in the central section of the story (i. 18–25) has his attention and interest fixed *simply and solely upon the single declaration, γεννηθεὶς ἐκ πνεύματος ἁγίου?*

(1) This γεννηθεὶς ἐκ πνεύματος ἁγίου is not of course a primary creed; it is, indeed, historically preceded by two—perhaps three—preparatory stages; but even for this very reason, as will be seen, it remains on the most primitive lines. The first stage is described by the formula reproduced by St Paul in Rom. i. 4: ὁ ὁρισθεὶς υἱὸς θεοῦ κατὰ πνεῦμα ἁγιωσύνης ἐξ ἀναστάσεως νεκρῶν: the second—if indeed we may count in this way—is given in the *Story of the Transfiguration* (οὗτός ἐστιν ὁ υἱός μου ὁ ἀγαπητός); the third in the *Story of the Baptism* (the Descent of the Spirit and ἐγὼ σήμερον γεγέννηκά σε). Their experience of the Resurrection at once firmly established the disciples in the faith that Jesus was *the Son of God proceeding from the Spirit of God.* Immediately, however, attempts began to be made to give some definite basis to this creed. Did He become Son of God at the Resurrection? No! but at the very first moment of His appearance on earth. But the latter idea did not displace the three others which maintained themselves in peaceful juxtaposition (indeed, they did not absolutely exclude one

another, seeing that it was a question of the outpouring of the Spirit which could happen again and again). However, the very fact that these views continued to exist side by side is a guarantee that the new view was not an intruder from the sphere of heathen mythology,[1] but a logical conclusion from the belief that our Lord was *God's Son by the operation of the Holy Spirit.* Now, it of course seems certain that St Paul never even thought of the Virgin Birth, but it is not thereby proved that this "working hypothesis" of the Faith had not already made its appearance in some Christian communities of the time of St Paul. The article of faith, "God's Son by the operation of the

[1] As, I am sorry to say, even Gunkel asserts in *Zum Religionsgesch. Verständniss des N.T.* (1903), S. 64 ff. One is not surprised that others do not trouble themselves about the special genesis of the Jewish-Christian idea, and fly at once to mythological explanations; but a theologian is surely bound to examine things more microscopically. The Jewish-Christian idea at its root has nothing whatever to do with mythology, and also in its later history every mythological taint was anxiously guarded against. Such efforts must, of course, have been vain as soon as people began to picture the event in the imagination. For a long period, however, the presence of the mythological element was involuntary, and the idea was kept in close touch with its Jewish origin. The original conception, "Of the Holy Spirit," where "Spirit" in Semitic is, as is well known, of the feminine gender, and therefore excludes all conceptions of sexual mythology, is not only not forgotten in the Greek gospel of the Hebrews, but has in many other quarters set a bridle upon the imagination. On the other hand, it is not to be denied that the ancient Oriental idea, that the Saviour was to be born of an unknown father, and that his mother would be a virgin, may have mingled itself in the faith of many when once speculative study of the Old Testament had referred Isaiah vii. to the origin of our Lord. On the whole question, *vide* Franckh, "Die Geburtsgesch. Jesu Christi im Lichte der altorientalischen Weltanschauung" (*Philothesia für P. Kleinert*, 1907, S. 201 ff.).

Holy Spirit," had its own peculiar logic; catechisms were not yet in existence; all those who called Jesus their Lord and believed that all that they venerated in Him was due to the influence of the Spirit, though their imagination, their logic, their gnosis might start them along totally different paths, were yet of one faith. The path, however, which led back from the Resurrection to the first beginnings of Jesus was certainly the simplest and most obvious. It may have been—indeed, probably it was—taken at once. A Mark, even a Paul, may have taken it and followed it to the end without feeling, either of them, impelled to state in set terms the conclusion—that the Spirit of God had a part in the conception of our Lord—either in the gospel of the one or in the epistles of the other. They perhaps regarded it as self-evident. St Paul, at all events, had much greater things to say concerning the Lord.

(2) But the conviction that our Lord was born of the Holy Spirit did not, according to Jewish ideas, involve the exclusion of an earthly father any more than of an earthly mother, although "ruaḥ" is feminine. Hence one may, indeed must, cherish very serious doubts as to whether the idea of the Virgin Birth would have ever made its appearance on Jewish soil *if it had not been for Isa. vii. 14.* What is it that lies at the basis of St Matt. i. 18–25? Simply two elements: (1) the conviction: *γεννηθεὶς ἐκ πνεύματος ἁγίου*: and (2) the passage in Isaiah: *ἰδοὺ ἡ παρθένος ἐν γαστρὶ ἕξει καὶ τέξεται υἱόν, καὶ καλέσουσιν τὸ ὄνομα αὐτοῦ* Εμμανουήλ. Many critics regard it as self-evident that this passage could not have been thus used until after the belief in

the Virgin Birth had already taken form; but such a view is by no means self-evident. It would only be self-evident if the origin of this belief on Jewish soil were a very simple matter, either because Jews had access to heathen mythology, or because the conviction that the Holy Spirit played a part in the origin of our Lord necessarily led to this conclusion. But neither of these conditions admits of demonstration[1]; indeed, it is easy to establish their opposite.

Zahn (in his Commentary on St Matthew) and others demand proof that at the time of our Lord this passage of Isaiah was interpreted of the Messiah; and they flaunt in one's face the fact that no Rabbi, so far as we know, has ever been led, because of Isa. vii., or any other reason, to suppose that the Messiah was to be born of a virgin. They are perhaps correct, but they overlook the fact that the situation had entirely changed for those who had become Christians. The faith that Jesus was born of the Ruaḥ of God necessarily opened up for these converts *new* sources of prophecy in the New Testament. *Δώσει κύριος αὐτὸς ὑμῖν σημεῖον!* With this majestic utterance Isaiah introduces the birth of Immanuel! To Christians themselves "the virgin" may at first have been as strange and embarrassing as the name "Immanuel"; but they were obliged to come to terms with them, for the promise, that to the nation which wearied its God would be given a sign whereby the believing part of the nation would find their Saviour, was too grand and too plainly

[1] The testimony adduced from Philo is without importance; besides, it is strangely out of place to bring in Philo here.

fulfilled to be passed by. *Therefore, Jesus was born of a virgin*, for so it is written! Here two objections may be raised; in the first place, it may be said that those who were capable of the train of thought which resulted in the idea of birth from a virgin, were also capable of directly adopting the myth of a virgin birth; and, secondly, we may be told that it is only in the Greek text of Isaiah that there is any mention of a virgin, whilst the original text at the very least left open the interpretation "young woman." But the reception of a myth demands quite different historical premisses from those which would explain how men could arrive at a conclusion, which looks like a myth, and yet really has nothing to do with mythology. A myth of this kind necessarily includes, not only a divine *father*, who is wanting here, but also a concrete directness in the treatment of detail which is likewise entirely absent here. It may be true that, even assuming that the belief was simply derived from the sacred text, still the very fact that men could come to believe that Jesus was born of a virgin by the operation of the Holy Spirit, in itself shows a disposition of mind that was not present among Jews a few generations earlier; but between such a disposition and the readiness simply to convert a heathen myth *in suum usum* [or, rather, to borrow its idea] there still yawns a gulf that cannot be bridged over. As for the objection that the word "virgin" stands only in the Greek text, it is not only probable that the combination which led to the belief originated among the Hellenistic Jews of Palestine (it is well known that a section of the strict Jewish Christians *always* refused to accept it), but it also seems probable to me that even in pre-Christian times many orthodox Jews, in the course of their brooding study of the original text of scripture, were led to the conclusion that Isa. vii. spoke of a virgin as the mother of the Messiah. Accordingly, neither the γεννηθεὶς ἐκ πνεύματος ἁγίου nor the Virgin Birth compel us to assume an advanced period in the development of Christian doctrine; on the contrary, these ideas, which have nothing to do with the idea of Pre-existence, are primitive in themselves, and are declared to be primitive by the fact that at the end of the first century, or at least the beginning of the second century, they were the *common property* of Christians, as St John (chap. i., according to the true text) and Ignatius teach us. But every belief which at that time was the common property of Christians (including the Palestinian churches) must be traced back to the churches of Palestine, and must be ascribed to the first decades after the Resurrection.

It is therefore beyond dispute that in the most important verses (i. 18–25) of the story of the Infancy in the first gospel nothing is to be found that could not have been written about the year 70 A.D.; and the analysis of the section which we have here undertaken has the advantage that it dispenses with all but two certain and clearly established factors—with the fact that the Church from the beginning ascribed what was characteristic in our Lord's personality to the special operation of the Holy Spirit, and with the passage from the Prophet Isaiah. If, however, in the end a conception made its appearance which converged with contemporary heathen mythological conceptions—we can only speak of convergence never of amalgamation in the Catholic Church—such a question belongs to the vast subject of the striking convergences of that syncretic epoch, which were at first, for the most part, involuntary.

The part of the story of the Infancy containing the genealogy and the Virgin Birth stands in no connection with the legend of the Magi.[1] The abode of Joseph and Mary in Egypt is perhaps historical; and yet it seems to me quite possible that such a legend, even if there were no fact behind it, could have taken form in the actual lifetime of the nearest relatives of our Lord; for the visit which it records lay far behind the personal recollection of the brothers of our Lord. Still, the process of the formation of the legend would be much simpler to understand if this incident were a fact.[2] Whether a fact of any kind lay at the founda-

[1] Chap. ii. 1 begins, without connecting with the preceding chapter, as an entirely new section, and seems to presuppose that the birth in Bethlehem had been previously narrated. We cannot tell how it was that this strange arrangement came about.

[2] In support of this we may be inclined also to appeal with some reserve to ancient Jewish legends about our Lord. On the other hand, we cannot overlook the likelihood that we have here a legend with a theological tendency parallel to the leading of the people of Israel out of Egypt. As for the birth in Bethlehem, the historian cannot go beyond the verdict "*non liquet.*" He cannot get rid of the suspicion that the story is due to Mic. v. 1; on the other hand, it is difficult to comprehend how the statement that Jesus was born in Bethlehem remained uncontradicted, if it was not a fact. But was it perhaps contradicted, and is it only we who have heard nothing of such a contradiction?

tion of the legend of the Magi is a matter quite beyond our ken. It is in itself by no means impossible that *μάγοι ἀπὸ ἀνατολῶν* once came to Jerusalem at the time of Herod, in order to acquire information concerning the Jewish Messiah in connection with some astronomical occurrence,[1] and it is also possible that the Massacre of the Innocents in Bethlehem has an historical nucleus of some kind[2]; but the story of the Magi is narrated with such a naïve disregard of all probability that the question whether the events really happened in the life of our Lord does not present itself to the historian. Here the first Evangelist has followed a legend that had taken form among a section of the people untouched by historical culture; it is, however, going too far to have recourse to the Diaspora, or even to Rome, for the origin of this legend, and to imagine that the story is based upon some Oriental embassage to the palace of the Cæsars. The "Star out of Jacob," combined with the presence of Chaldæan astrologers in Jerusalem, is quite sufficient. As to the question how early or how late such a folk-tale could have made its appearance in Jewish-Christian circles no sensible person

[1] The story of the Magi is not deduced from prophecy; for in it no reference is made to prophecy. The legend obviously contains an accusation against Herod and the leaders of the people; it is aggressive, not apologetic. Whether it is intended to forecast the idea of the Gentile Church is at least doubtful; rather it seems, without any special bias, to aim at the glorification of our Lord.

[2] As a simple invention from prophecy the legend seems very crass. We, however, have no means that would enable us to give an assured judgment on this point.

will care to give a definite answer in the present state of our knowledge.

Among the passages peculiar to St Matthew the sections xvi. 17 ff. and xviii. 15 ff. strike one as betraying a later date. They do not, however, come into consideration in connection with our question whether the gospel was written some years earlier or later. If we are convinced that these sections are of relatively early date, and that they belong to Palestinian tradition, then they can be just as well assigned to the period before as to the period after 60 or 70 A.D. If, however, one agrees with many critics in the opinion that they are of a much later date, then one must take into consideration the probability that they simply do not belong to the original content of the gospel and are to be regarded as later interpolations.[1] In regard to xvi. 17 ff. the latter opinion is the more probable in that we are here altogether unprepared for the mention of the Church and for the promise of its impregnability. If impregnability is to be mentioned, we should rather expect a promise that St Peter would at the last stand firm against the assault of Hell. Indeed, ancient commentators have interpreted the passage as if it ran: *οὐ κατισχύσουσίν σου*, and perhaps it did once run thus; *cf.* Tatian (while the words: *καὶ ἐπὶ ταύτῃ τῇ πέτρᾳ οἰκοδομήσω μου τὴν ἐκκλησίαν* were also wanting).

The remaining stories peculiar to St Matthew are all connected with the Crucifixion and the Resurrection of our Lord. Among these the stories of the death of

[1] Hence the date of the gospel ought not to be made to depend upon them.

Judas, of Pilate's wife,[1] and of Pilate and the people, contain nothing that could not have been already related at a very early date. In particular, xxvii. 7 presupposes that both the author and the first readers knew the situation of the "Field of Blood," near Jerusalem, which was formerly called "The Potter's Field." The tradition thus originated in Jerusalem, and it is easier to suppose that it arose before the destruction of the city. Again, the quite isolated and altogether extraordinary story of those who rose from the dead at the moment of our Lord's death (they, moreover, appear to many in the Holy City) seems to me to be primitive; for on dogmatic grounds each successive decade would only raise a more and more strenuous protest against its appearance. The legends of the Resurrection contain a decidedly late piece of tradition in the story (xxviii. 9, 10) that our Lord appeared to the women on their return from the sepulchre. However, not only on internal but also on external grounds[2] this passage may be judged not to belong to the original content of the gospel, and therefore gives no information concerning the date of its composition. The concluding passage (xxviii. 16 ff.), recording the appearance of the Risen Christ to His disciples in *Galilee*, is ancient tradition; it is, however, doubtful whether the words spoken by our Lord belong

[1] The intervention of the wife of the judge in favour of the delinquent is a trait which, as is shown by the stories of the persecutions, is often historical, often also fictitious.

[2] Verse 11 connects closely with verse 8; accordingly the verses 9 and 10 appear to be interpolated. They are, besides, a doublet to verses 6 and 7.

to the original gospel. The declaration "ἐδόθη μοι πᾶσα ἐξουσία ἐν οὐρανῷ καὶ ἐπὶ γῆς" has a very different sound from Matt. xi. 27: πάντα μοι παρεδόθη ὑπὸ τοῦ πατρός μου":[1] neither is there anything in the content of the gospel that prepares us for the succeeding passage. If, however, these passages must be accounted to belong to the original gospel, then there is nothing either in the general missionary commission or in the Trinitarian formula that would prevent our assigning them to the period before the destruction of Jerusalem. The Trinitarian formula was not a creation of St Paul, but was already adopted by him from the Jewish Christians.[2] Finally, the stories of the Watch at the Sepulchre and of the Angel (xxvii. 62–66; xxviii. 2 ff. 11–15) are apologetical devices which could have come into use very early in the history of the controversy with the Jews, especially if the Watch at the Sepulchre may be regarded as historical. A "custodia" of this kind over the bodies of executed persons is also mentioned elsewhere; *cf.* the Martyrs of Lyons in Euseb., v. i. 59: ἀτάφους παρεφύλαττον μετὰ στρατιωτικῆς ἐπιμελείας ἡμέραις συχναῖς. Accordingly, there is nothing in the narratives peculiar to St Matthew that can disturb our confidence in the date we have been led to assign to that gospel.

Passing on to the consideration of the passages peculiar to St Luke, we are at first confronted with the long story of the Infancy, chaps. i., ii., iii. 23–38. I cannot here produce the proof that this passage not

[1] *Scil.*, all knowledge of God, all παράδοσις.

[2] *Vide* my *Kirchenverfassung* (1910), S. 187 ff.

only depends upon two main sources, but also proceeds in the last instance from two distinct religious strata[1]; for the story of the infancy of the Baptist, which even now bears upon the face of it that it was not originally intended to serve as an introduction to the history of our Lord, must have originated in the circle of the disciples of St John (i. 5–25, 46–55, 57–80); and it is also evident that iii. 1 ff. (so far as fresh tradition is here added to St Mark and Q) is derived from the same circle.[2] The passage i. 39–45, 56 binds together the two entirely independent stories, the first of which celebrated the Baptist, not as the forerunner of the Messiah Jesus, but as the preparer of the way for the coming of Jahweh the Saviour (i. 16, 17). The story of St John's infancy is thus very ancient, and presents the tradition of the disciples of St John in Lukan dress. The story of the infancy of our Lord comes from quite

[1] [The translator may perhaps be allowed to refer to a work of his, in which the question of the two sources and of the Johannine character of one of these is dealt with in detail. *A Johannine Document in the Third Gospel*, Luzac, 1902.]

[2] Is it too much to suppose that St Luke, before he joined the Christian community, was an adherent of the disciples of the Baptist, and had even at that time made historical studies, which he at a later date made use of for his gospel? The attitude which he adopts in the gospel (also in the Acts) towards the disciples of the Baptist and the "Spirit" suggests this question. There is yet another point. In the clause (iii. 15), *προσδοκῶντος τοῦ λαοῦ καὶ διαλογιζομένων πάντων ἐν ταῖς καρδίαις αὐτῶν περὶ τοῦ 'Ιωάννου, μή ποτε αὐτὸς εἴη ὁ Χριστός*, St Luke has probably reproduced his own experiences, which, after the narrative of chap. i., are very intelligible. This narrative can only proceed from the circle of the Baptist, and only one who stood in close relationship with this circle could have used it to introduce the history of our Lord.

different circles from those whence sprang the corresponding story in St Matthew. Interest in Joseph is here almost entirely wanting. St Mary is, on the other hand, thrust into the foreground; *vide* i. 26–45, 56; ii. 5, 16, 19, 33–35, 48, 51; indeed, from ii. 19, 51 it follows that the stories are intended to be regarded as derived in the last instance from St Mary herself. Here we are, of course, destitute of all means of historical control, and there can be no doubt that these stories have been freely edited by a poetic artist, namely, St Luke. But there can be just as little doubt that St Luke regarded them as proceeding from St Mary; for his practice elsewhere as an historian proves that he could not have himself invented a fiction like this. Hence we may conclude that they came to him claiming the authority of St Mary, and therefore certainly from Palestine. The only question that interests us here is whether such stories conflict with the date we have been led to assign to the third gospel.[1] No one will maintain that they directly favour so early a date; and yet, on the other hand, it is quite impossible to contend that they directly conflict with our date.

[1] The stories are essentially homogeneous in character. The circle whence they proceed had the most profound veneration for St Mary, and placed her next her Son in a position of great importance. Such feelings do not arise of themselves, they must go back to the impression made by the personality of St Mary herself. A poet under the influence of this impression, with poetic licence, has transferred to the time of the Conception and of the Birth what really belonged to the inward life of the mother of our Lord at a later period. During His lifetime our Lord found no faith in His own family. It seems to me almost impossible to imagine that this poet was at work before the death of St Mary.

Nothing that is mythological in the sense of Greek or Oriental myth is to be found in these accounts; all here is in the spirit of the Old Testament, and most of it reads like a passage from the historical books of that ancient volume. As for parallels with ancient stories of gods and heroes, it would be treating them too seriously to describe them as scanty and feeble, and no one hitherto has been able to raise them above the sphere of the purely accidental. Seeing that we know so little of St Mary, not even, in spite of all the legends, how long she lived, we have absolutely no fixed point upon which to base the discussion of the question: How it is that she could have been made responsible for these stories? From Acts i. 14 we receive the latest historical information about her. There is a certain probability in favour of the view that St Philip and his daughters transmitted to St Luke gospel traditions—perhaps these stories were included among them. The very large number of new features which St Luke has in common with the fourth gospel in no instance suggests to the critic that these features must have been conceived after the destruction of Jerusalem, or, at least, after the year 60 A.D. Together with much that is questionable they include a great deal that is free from objection, and accordingly historical; hence we may regard them, though foreign to St Mark, as ancient tradition of Palestinian origin.

Passing over the narratives v. 4–9 (St Peter's draught of fishes), vii. 36–50 (the woman who was a sinner), xi. 27 f. (the woman's cry of joy over the mother of our Lord), which are neutral in regard to the question of the date of the third gospel,[1] we forthwith arrive at the incidents peculiar to St Luke in the history of the Crucifixion and of the Resurrection. But here, also, the accounts xxiii. 6–12, 27–31, 34, 39–43, 46, though they give rise to serious doubt, do not permit any conclusions as to the date of the gospel.[2] Hence we are only left with the question whether the stories of the Resurrection (including the Ascension) enter a protest against an early date for the twofold work.

Here everything really reduces itself to the single question whether the idea that the apparitions of the Risen Christ in and near Jerusalem were the first apparitions could have made its appearance during the first generation after the death of our Lord. The question does not exist for those critics who, like Zahn, Loofs, and others, believe that these apparitions were actually the first; but seeing that these scholars allow that the accounts in St Mark and St Matthew presuppose apparitions, or a single apparition, in Galilee as the first, they too acknowledge the reality of the difficulty that, even before the destruction of Jerusalem, different opinions already prevailed concerning the locality of the first apparition of our Lord. In fact, it must be acknowledged that controversy on this point goes back to the earliest times, indeed, that there was perhaps never a time when Christendom was firmly and

[1] The story of the Draught of Fishes is also neutral, even if, as is probable, it is not correctly placed in St Luke, but belongs to the narratives of the Resurrection.

[2] The story of "Jesus and Herod" *may* be historical; St Luke possessed, as his work shows, special sources of information on this theme.

unanimously agreed upon this point. Taking even our four gospels, we shall find that each of them, if they are closely studied, conceals a double account, and in addition we have many other ancient and conflicting authorities. The following summary will here be instructive[1]:—

1. A source of St Luke (xxiv. 34): St Peter was the first to see the Lord (where? when?).

2. St Paul (1 Cor. xv. 5): St Peter was the first to see the Lord, then the Twelve (where? when?).

3. The conjectural original of St Mark (*vide* xiv. 28; xvi. 7): St Peter and the other disciples were the first to see the Lord, and this in Galilee,[2] after the third day.

4. The gospel of St Peter: St Peter and some other disciples (among them Levi the son of Alphæus) were the first to see the Lord in Galilee while they were fishing, after the third day.

5. The source of St John xxi. (undoubtedly intended originally as an account of the first appearance of our Lord): St Peter and some other disciples were the first to see the Lord in Galilee as they were fishing [it is, moreover, probable that the stories of two appearances are intertwined in St John xxi.].

6. The gospel of St Matthew [without xxviii. 9, 10]: the eleven disciples were the first to see the Lord on a mountain in Galilee, after the third day.

[1] *Cf.* my treatise, "Ein jüngst entdeckter Auferstehungsbericht," in *Der Festschrift für B. Weiss* (1897).

[2] The efforts which have been repeated lately by Lepsius and Resch, jun., to discover "Galilee" in Judæa, near to Jerusalem, have not convinced me.

7. The gospel of St John: St Mary Magdalene was the first to see the Lord, beside the empty tomb, on the morning of the third day.

8. The spurious conclusion of St Mark (Aristion?): the same as St John.

9. The interpolation in St Matthew (xxviii. 9 f.): St Mary Magdalene and another Mary were the first to see the Lord by the way on their return from the empty tomb.

10. *Didasc. Apost.*: Levi was the first among the disciples to see the Lord after He had appeared to St Mary Magdalene and the other Mary.

11. Hippol., *Comm. in Cantic.*: Mary and Martha were the first to see the Lord.

12. Tatian (*Ephraem. Diodor.*): St Mary the mother of our Lord was the first to see Him.

13. The gospel of St Luke: two disciples (Cleopas and another unnamed) were the first to see the Lord at Emmaus, near Jerusalem, towards the evening of the third day.

14. The gospel of the Hebrews: James the Just was the first to see the Lord on the morning of the third day.

Though these opposing witnesses are by no means of equal weight, yet even those of later date testify that this vacillation in testimony goes back to the earliest period. We may evidently conclude therefrom that the question soon became a purely party question, and that even the Primitive Church of Jerusalem very soon lost a certain and uncontroverted tradition both in regard to the person who was the first to see the Lord as well as in regard to the locality of the first appearance. Appearances occurred very soon both in and near Jerusalem, as well as in Galilee, and—the fact of the empty grave being assumed—it almost necessarily followed that a legend should grow up telling that the finding of the empty tomb was at once accompanied by an appearance, especially if, as is very probable, appearances at the empty tomb actually took place very shortly afterwards. The factor of the empty tomb complicated and disturbed the tradition of the appearances. The view that variation in the accounts did not arise until after 60 or 70 A.D. is altogether improbable; for if the statement, "Jesus first of all appeared to Peter in Galilee," had continued to be an unquestioned article of faith during the first thirty years, it is quite incomprehensible how doubt could have then arisen, *i.e.* how another account could have come into existence. However, for the question which now concerns us, it is sufficient to establish this one point, namely, that though St Luke is found to contradict St Mark and St Matthew in his stories of the Resurrection, we may not therefore conclude that he must have written after 60 or 70 A.D. Again, the tradition as to the history of the Crucifixion and Resurrection, which St Luke shares in common with the fourth gospel, appears with characteristic variation in the two evangelists; hence it must itself belong to a much earlier period. But even in the original form of this tradition the scene of the appearances had been already transferred to Jerusalem.

We have still to consider the difference between the

first and second works of St Luke in what they record concerning the abode of our Lord on earth after His Resurrection and concerning the Ascension. Even the gospel pictures our Lord taking a solemn farewell from the disciples, and it places the scene at Bethany; the Acts, however, declares that the solemn farewell took place after forty days during which the disciples were systematically instructed by our Lord, that the scene of the farewell was the Mount of Olives, and that our Lord ascended into Heaven before the eyes of the disciples. What is distinctly new and interesting in this tradition is not the corporal Ascension, together with the accompanying angels—a story like this could have easily taken form as soon as the Twelve were scattered abroad,—but the forty days' converse of our Lord with His disciples. We may declare, without a shadow of a doubt, that not only St Paul, St Mark, and St Matthew, but even St Luke himself in his gospel, as well as St John, exclude such a story. On the other hand, we must not fail to notice that the beginnings of such a tradition are to be found only in St Luke, namely, in the story of the Journey to Emmaus (especially xxiv. 27–32) and in a slighter degree in St John xx., xxi. The Acts gives us no stories of events happening during this time of converse. It is therefore evident that the *period of time* itself is alone significant. This must be due to some speculation of Messianic and apocalyptic character, and is accordingly a theologumenon which could be combined with any historical reminiscence. Probably at first it had nothing to do with the converse of the Risen Christ with His disciples, but was thought of as a period of waiting and preparation before the investure with the Heavenly Messiahship; the number "40" points to such an explanation. Hence the idea itself may well be primitive. Our conclusion from this survey is therefore:[1] that we have found nothing to upset the verdict, to which we have been led by critical investigation of the Acts of the Apostles, that the second and third gospels, as well as the Acts, were composed while St Paul was still alive, and that the first gospel came into being only a few years later.

[1] I am well aware that the discussion in the last pages is of a very summary character; but it gives the quintessence of a thorough investigation. I was able to be brief because, apart from the story of the Infancy of our Lord, the subjects discussed have not been the object of systematic criticism and hypothesis of a character hostile to my results. At least, I know of no treatise which expressly bases conclusive arguments for bringing the synoptic gospels down to the end of the first century upon definite narratives which they contain. People are satisfied with showing that these gospels presuppose the destruction of Jerusalem, that the standpoint of their authors is "post-Pauline," and that they show the traces of subsequent experiences of the Church; but whether these subsequent experiences belong to the period between 30 and 60 A.D., or to some later time—this is a question which is almost never raised, and for good reasons, because definite evidence upon which to decide it is wanting.